Liturgical Lockdown

Liturgical Lockdown

Covid and the Absence of the Laity

A New Zealand Perspective

J.P. Grayland

All scriptural references from New International Version.

All references to documents of the Second Vatican Council: A. Flannery, ed., The Basic Sixteen Documents, Vatican II, Constitutions, Decrees, Declarations (New York, Dublin: Costello Publishing and Dominican Publications,1996).

Table of Contents

Acknowledgments

The book's genesis is a series of articles published in La Croix International during 2020 and early 2021 that reflected the liturgical change throughout 2020.

I wish to thank a great group of friends and colleagues who helped with suggestions and reading the various drafts.

I am grateful to all my Kotahi Ano Pastoral Team colleagues for their work during the Covid lockdown.

INTRODUCTION

In 2020, and again in 2021, the New Zealand Catholic Church lost the sacred physical space where we celebrate the Eucharist. We lost the presence of the laity at Sunday Mass and turned to online media. Covid-19 brought an abrupt end to our patterns of social interaction and worship. Because it changed our physical and social interaction patterns, it changed our foundational understanding of the liturgical community. Covid-19 disrupted established worshipping communities and hierarchies. As a result, we created alternative forms of worship and sacramental mediation. Covid introduced a new term to liturgical theology: "liturgical lockdown".

By recounting our story of disruption and innovation, I hope to show the pastoral and liturgical upheaval it brought and how we sought to address it. It is a narrative of one combined parish's response to this unique time of change. The focus on adaptation and innovation of liturgical rituals during Covid has modified our liturgical behaviours and pastoral presumptions.

Liturgical lockdown brought our habitual patterns of worship to an abrupt halt. It changed the way Catholics, among many believers, gather for worship and fellowship. Lockdown radically altered our presumptions of pastoral ministry and our normative patterns of communication and community. Most importantly, it changed our foundational assumptions of the sacramental-liturgical assembly. The Covid experience introduced a new way of being a community and a strong aversion to physical gatherings, of which the Church is one.

One year on from the liturgical lockdown of Easter 2020, we celebrated in 2021 Holy Week and the Paschal Triduum without any restrictions. The experience underpinning this book is the experience in New Zealand. We are very aware of other countries and their struggle with Covid-19. For example, our large and growing Indian and Filipino communities have been very concerned by the situation in their home nation. We have supported them with words and prayers. Just before Easter 2021, a good friend in Gelsenkirchen, Germany, who had booked a seat for Easter Sunday Mass with her son, texted me and asked: "you still remember what it is like to be in lockdown?" The answer was no! I had forgotten because I had become busy again with life. The "new normal" of doing things looks very much like the "old normal" except in one significant way—we are different.

In August 2021, New Zealand returned to level four lockdown. This experience after a year of freedom was another taste of disruption, but this time we were ready for it. Again, the churches were closed, and our formal sacramental and liturgical life was suspended, and our social life was home-based. We returned to the online environment and produced online prayer resources. Email, text, the internet, and the phone became the primary tools to communicate with parishioners and stay visible. We were not adapting on the run as we had in March and April 2020. In 2021 I sensed a different approach to lockdown. In 2020 we had been the compliant and obedient team of five million, enthusiastically sharing our hardship and staying at home; the world was quiet. In 2021, the lockdown was different. There was more traffic on the roads, it was noisier, and the lockdown was more tedious.

The context of my reflection is Aotearoa, New Zealand, where we have lived in relative safety longer than most countries. This contextual perspective does not reflect all countries and local churches. The uniqueness of the context offers a view that I hope will provide the reader with another perspective from which to consider their own context's opportunities and challenges. The book's content and direction reflect my experience of Covid disruption in our three cooperating parishes, which comprise two city parishes and one country parish. I work in a pastoral team of nine, four of whom are part-time, two are full-time, five are laywomen, and three are priests. During the 2020 lockdown, the Cathedral presbytery was home to three priests and one deacon. Although our experience of lockdown and disruption to parish liturgical and pastoral life is local and particular, it reflects a more extensive pattern across New Zealand. Social lockdown brought sudden, unexpected changes to our liturgical and pastoral practices.

In a liturgically divided Church, I approach the question of the place of the laity in liturgy from the position of Pauline liturgical theology and practice as articulate in the theology and rites of the Second Vatican Council. From this perspective, I ask why the response of virtual masses became the dominant response of clergy. I ask it because I understand liturgy as the work of the entire Church, the People of God.

What you read throughout is my *reflection-in-action*, *reflection-on-action*, and *reflection-on-being-reformed*. These three reflections overlap and are seen in the way material is presented. Before the experience of Covid, I had never experienced Easter without the Paschal Triduum or Sundays without Mass. Neither had I experienced the loss of the sacred physical place we call a church and the more important sacred physical space we call the Sunday Liturgy. These were simply presumed. Before Covid, I never thought I would see funerals in churches forbidden. I did not expect to be classified as a non-essential worker, yet all this happened! It was a clarion statement of the status of religion and religious ministry in the modern, liberal democracy of New Zealand. While some Catholics responded negatively, others saw it as a necessary step.

Reflection-in-action looks at the experience of constructing new practices and facing further theological change in an unpredictable environment. To illustrate this, I tell the story of how our parishes amended their pastoral outreach and developed new lines of communication and pastoral presence. Underlying this reflection are the following questions: What is going on here? What is being communicated, and why do we need to communicate so much? What does this new drive to communicate say about us as Catholics, and was it essential before Covid?

Reflection-on-action is the thinking back into the experience of liturgical lockdown to gain new knowledge and insight into our presumptive operational theologies to come to a new understanding of how to minister in a new epoch. The virtual Mass is the prominent example here that needs to be discussed because it was our dominant response during the liturgical lockdown. Underpinning this reflection are the following questions: What does liturgical lockdown signify for us in this place and time? What does it mean for our religious living when we cannot pray in common? What is at stake through not being able to gather, pray, and work together? What does virtual Mass tell us about ourselves and our approach to liturgy, religion, and priesthood?

Reflection-on-being-reformed through the experience of change locates this book. I, like everyone else, experienced the liturgical lockdown, and like everyone else, I was forced to respond to a sudden change that was beyond my control. This reflection acknowledges the need to engage with our rich and vibrant Catholic liturgical and sacramental traditions and ask, have we aligned our responses during Covid-19 to these traditions and used them to help us navigate the chaos, or have we abandoned them for a foundationally different default setting?

In the context of *reflection-in-action, reflection-on-action,* and *reflection-on-being-reformed,* I will develop throughout the book four key themes: (1) disruption, (2) virtual or online worship, (3) active participation in the liturgy, and (4) the theology of the laity in liturgy, because these four themes marked the liturgical experience of lockdown, and they will continue to be determiners of change in the liturgical reform initiated through Covid-19.

My conclusions come from four surveys I completed during 2020 and 2021. I asked respondents how they experienced virtual masses and their value. I followed this with a survey to priests in 2021, where I asked them if they offered virtual masses and why. As well as these, I have used personal stories, discussion group material, and researched international online sources that have discussed the liturgical responses during the liturgical lockdown.

The book is divided into six parts. Part One, *Disruption and Innovation*, Part Two, *Liturgical Theology*, Part Three, *Virtual Liturgy*, Part Four,

Technology and Liturgy, Part Five *Mediated Sacraments* and Part Six *Competing Liturgical Theologies.* It concludes with *Not a Conclusion.*

Part One outlines our parish's experience of liturgical and pastoral disruption during the first significant lockdown of 2020. Using Clayton Christensen's term disruptive innovation from his 1997 book *The Innovator's Dilemma,* [1] I approach the experience of lockdown as a period of rapid disruption and innovation of our pastoral, liturgical, sacramental, and social lives. We have experienced disruption and innovation with an immediacy that is rarely known outside wartime. The purpose of this section is to consider the nature and impact of Covid-19 as an agent of both disruption and innovation on our pastoral, sacramental and liturgical lives.

Our story illustrates the work many parishes did to remain in contact with parishioners and meet the challenges of moving to a technological mindset. Like everyone else, the priest was a "locked-down" non-essential worker, so liturgical lockdown also meant pastoral lockdown and the need to readjust our concepts and practices of pastoral ministry and outreach. As our liturgical and pastoral life came to a sudden halt, we experienced the rare challenge of a non-functioning mediated sacramental system. I explore the impact of social distancing on our community for whom physical gathering, in whatever form, became the danger.

Part Two presents a theology of the liturgy and liturgical praxis that is central to my argument against the use of virtual masses and for the place of the laity in liturgical prayer, especially the Sunday Mass. I explore the operative theology that supports the use of virtual masses through online systems and why I think this operative theology is problematic.

Part Three considers the virtual Mass, which many think is a great innovation, but I hope to show that the virtual Mass is not as innovative as one might think. Our communication forms are changing. The high uptake of digital worship during Covid reflects the equally high uptake of digital family gatherings. Virtual masses represent a mirroring of contemporary social connection and a transition towards it.

In Part Four, I look at what I think is the most significant disruption to the experience of liturgy, the loss of safety and access to physical gatherings through social distancing. The loss of the physical, social gathering has brought the loss of the sacred physical space and its sacred place. In this part, I look critically at the nature and the place of the assembly in Catholic worship and the impact of technology on the liturgy of the Eucharist.

In Part Five, I look at the issues of a mediated sacramental system when it loses its physicality and proximate presence. The loss of these essential elements has brought our mediated, sacramental system to a grinding halt, and as a result, we have looked around for solutions that do not satisfy. At the end of Part Five, I consider the impact of Covid on the sacraments of Reconciliation, the Anointing of the Sick and Home-Eucharists.

In Part Six, I offer an assessment of the competing liturgical-sacramental models of liturgy that play a role in the contemporary church and our responses to liturgical lockdown. The experience we have come to call liturgical lockdown has exposed the underlying operative theology that effortlessly enabled the Mass to move to the virtual platform. This operative theology lies deep in the psyche of inherited patterns of worship and priesthood, driving our liturgical and pastoral responses. I conclude Part Six with *Seven Considerations* for your assessment and reflection.

Finally, in the conclusion that is not a conclusion, I draw together various strands and end with more questions than answers because the Covid-19 experience is unpredictable. Some changes are observable now, and others will take years, or decades, to become apparent. This final section offers my concluding questions because the pandemic continues to wreak havoc across the globe. Many people still cannot gather for worship in their faith tradition or safely go shopping. The second lockdown in 2021 in Aotearoa, New Zealand, suggests the longer-term impact of the Covid-liturgical experience is instability and change. The liturgical reform through Covid-19 is significant because it is not mandated by the Church but by a virus, politics, public health, and government legislation. In the context of Covid-19, we gain an insight into the drivers of liturgical and pastoral reform akin to those brought by the plagues of medieval Europe.

Sacrosanctum Concilium is my starting point for considering the impact of the liturgical reform brought through liturgical disruption and virtual worship to active and conscious participation by the laity in the liturgical prayer of the Church. *Sacrosanctum Concilium* shapes my understanding of the Church's post-conciliar vision because it places liturgy front and centre in the work of salvation. Because of this central place, the liturgical act is the outpouring of God. Thus, it must be accessible to all people in its authentic form because 'in the liturgy the sanctification of women and men is given expression in symbols perceptible by the sense and is carried out in ways appropriate to each of them.'[2] *Sacrosanctum Concilium* shapes the post-conciliar worldview, or at least it should.

Throughout the book, my central question is the theological meaning of the place of the laity in the celebration of the Mass. My paramount concern is that virtual or online masses have side-lined the laity, reducing them—theologically—to passive, non-essential participants, promoting a liturgical culture of passivity. It begs the question, why did we do this? Why did we respond to the pandemic by reducing our most sacred action to an online product? Why did we search around the scrap bins of worship—rather than suffer the truth that we could not gather—and offer our people an artificial form of leitourgia?

My reflection on the role and response of the clergy is based on a focus group, multiple conversations, and interviews with priests in New Zealand and a survey in May 2021. What happened in the psyche of the clergy during lockdown is crucial because it contributed to the proliferation of the virtual Mass. The clergy response also indicates an operative theology present in the contemporary priesthood.

Who is this book's audience? The audience is anyone interested in the liturgy as a transformative event and who struggles with it as a transactional event and those questioning the value and the future of the virtual Mass through online systems. I would ask you to keep four questions in mind as you read. The first is, "when the people are not present at worship as active, physical participants, has the Church gathered and celebrated the Eucharist?" The second question is, "does the virtual Mass express the operative theology in Catholicism because it rejects the laity's active participation in the Mass?" And the third is "is the transactional notion of the priest as the surrogate of the people before God at the heart of our operative theology?"

These three questions are asked against the backdrop of Covid-19's unique set of circumstances. Like other organisations, we were totally unprepared for Covid. Nonetheless, to answer the three preceding questions, I must ask you to consider a fourth: "are the instances of virtual Mass, the priest saying Mass alone, walk-up holy communion, online adoration and spiritual communion all examples of a pre-conciliar catholic culture to which we have simple reverted?" Your answers to the first three questions will determine how you answer the fourth.

The Church lives out of the celebration of the sacraments, and the Eucharist is central. It is the source and summit, but what becomes of it, and us, when it is inaccessible? When the mediator is not present, what are the alternatives for Christians using a mediated sacramental system?

We have a thirst for prayer, which is our thirst for God. Acknowledging the suffering of the Covid lockdown, it is still essential to ask: What are we doing when we reduce our central sacramental action to a TV show and a drive-through communion stall? Is it just a seeming lack of imagination, or is it a window into something else?

I write about the Mass and the Eucharist throughout this book and occasionally use them interchangeably. At points, I ask or imply the question: is our need for the Mass equitable to our need for Eucharist? Can we distinguish between "saying the Mass" and "celebrating the Eucharist" enough for us to understand our own motivations when it comes to Sunday worship? The point of the question is: has our own need to hear and say

Mass overridden the purpose of eucharistic praise and thanksgiving? This is dangerous ground because it may give you the impression that I am doubting the Mass, the sacraments, and the priesthood—I am not, but I am asking: are we using these *as tools* to avoid suffering Covid?

I admit it is a fine line distinguishing between the "saying of Mass" and the "celebrating of the Eucharist", but I ask it because I am concerned that where praise becomes functional, it loses its transformational quality. It is true that people devotedly "hear" Mass and priests devotedly "say" Mass, but I think these two forms of "hearing" and "saying" belie a functional approach to worship. Equally, people may "celebrate Eucharist" and priests "preside at Eucharist" without a transformative mentality or awareness. Nevertheless, I think that to "celebrate Eucharist" and "preside at Eucharist" are more likely to be transformative than transactional.

I use the terms online and virtual interchangeably. Where I distinguish between virtual and online, I am drawing a distinction between the functionality of online, digital, or cyber communications and the experience of virtuality, or between the virtual and physical environments.

---

1 Clayton M. Christensen, The Innovator's Dilemma. When New Technologies Cause Great Firms to Fail, Harvard Business Review Press, (Boston, Massachusetts). First published in 1997, 2016, 323.
2 A. Flannery, ed., The Basic Sixteen Documents, Vatican II, Constitutions, Decrees, Declarations (New York, Dublin: Costello Publishing and Dominican Publications,1996). Sacrosanctum Concilium, 7, 121. Hereafter SC.

PART ONE
DISRUPTION AND INNOVATION

Disruption and Innovation

isruptive innovation is not a common theological or liturgical term. In fact, it is a business term coined by Clayton Christensen and made famous in his *The Innovator's Dilemma*. [1] He writes that successful companies are caught in the dilemma when they listen to their established customer base and invest in new technologies to meet this group's needs. In doing so, they unwittingly fail because they have listened to their dominant customer's demands and introduced new technologies to satisfy their demands. It seems a "no-win" situation for managers.

In seeking to be successful, companies introduce innovations to meet their mainstream customer's demands that Christensen describes as "sustaining technologies". These innovations sustain the dominant market and the mainstream customers and may even be used later by smaller, disruptive providers.

In the automotive industry, introducing a hybrid engine to upgrade a car model could be a sustaining technology because it adds the perception of value. It does not necessarily move a customer from the combustion engine to an electric engine because the hybrid car owner is still, essentially, a combustion engine devotee.

Sustaining innovations do not move the customer base forwards. In the end, the sustaining technology loses out to the genuinely revolutionary innovation of nuclear fusion engines lurking behind the movement to alternative engine types.

Christensen characterises disruptive technologies as those that change the value proposition. They almost always offer lower performance in terms of mainstream customers care about when they first appear.[2] Innovator companies can meet their customers' current needs and anticipate their future ones without in the process becoming obsolete. Disruptive innovation focuses on technologies and 'the transference of labor, capital, material and information into products and services of greater value'.[3] Innovation is a change in one of these technologies. The innovator's dilemma is seen in 'the processes through which disruptive technologies supplant older technologies and the powerful forces within well-managed companies that make them unlikely to develop those technologies themselves.'[4]

While many would say, the Catholic Church is an organisation incapable of anticipating the future needs of its people and innovating to meet them, a closer reading of Church history shows that the Church is constantly innovating in the face of disruption. The recent experience of Covid-19's disruption and innovation is being experienced with an immediacy that is rarely experienced known outside of wartime. This section focuses on the impact of disruption and innovation on our pastoral, sacramental and liturgical lives.

On the face of the virtual Mass looks to be the prominent disruption to worship, but I hope to show that the virtual Mass is not as innovative as one might think. Instead, the main force of disruption has been limiting physical gatherings and social distancing because these are seen as high-risk activities. The loss of physical gathering and social proximity has changed our broader social patterns of community, gathering, and travel and our concept of liturgy, church, and pastoral interaction. These more extensive social changes have disrupted our pastoral, sacramental and liturgical lives by losing physical, sacramental mediation. They are already changing our understanding of ministry, public prayer and pastoral work and pastoral management. As a result, we must rethink our fundamental theological presumptions of liturgy and pastoral work as a shared, physical, communal experience and fellowship. I hope that a brief look at Christensen's concept of disruptive innovation will help us understand the nature of the disruptive change we are experiencing and consider the future impacts of our innovations. But first, the story of our experience of liturgical and pastoral lockdown, social distancing and church closures and the sustaining technologies we used.

Our Story

In March 2020, New Zealand entered a period of Level Four lockdown that lasted for six weeks. In many other countries, this situation continued throughout 2020 and into 2021. During that time of social lockdown, religion was "non-essential". New Zealand clergy of all denominations and thousands of others were classified as non-essential workers, and places of worship were closed to the public. Like others deemed non-essential", the clergy were not permitted to enter their place of work—churches—throughout the lockdown. Neither were they allowed to visit hospitals and rest homes or bury the dead; this was left to funeral directors.

Once the highest level of lockdown was lifted, churches did not open because gatherings were restricted to ten people. When congregations of one hundred were allowed, most churches opened for services with strict physical distancing rules and sign-in protocols. Finally, when the restrictions on the number of people at public gatherings were increased and then removed, worship resumed in each diocese, but life did not go back to normal. The habitual patterns of worship and parish life had been broken, and parishioners returned slowly to worship.

Again, in mid-August 2020, New Zealand went back into Level Four. All church services—excluding funerals—stopped again and remained for several weeks in most parts of the country and longer in Auckland, New Zealand's largest city. When other parts of the country opened up again with congregations limited to one hundred, we also had sanitising routines and 'track and trace' processes for everyone attending Mass or visiting a church. We cordoned off sections of pews to ensure physical distancing between congregants. Most of our person-to-person ministry, such as communion to the sick, stopped again, and many forms of chaplaincy to prisons, hospitals and schools ceased. When groups of first ten and then fifty people could gather indoors, we gathered only for funerals and masses were suspended. At each level, public gatherings were a casualty of Covid. While at Level Four, all public gatherings were prohibited. At Level Three, a gathering of up to ten people was permitted, and Level Two, gatherings of 100 were permitted with restrictions.

On August 17, 2021, New Zealand entered a second extended lockdown that continued at various levels into October 2021. Ironically two days before on Sunday, August 15, the Feast of the Assumption, the New Zealand Catholic Bishops had rededicated the country to Our Lady's protection against Covid-19. The 2021 lockdown was a different experience throughout the country and especially in Auckland, where the lockdown was longer. On September 20, we held our first church gathering with 100 participants. It was vigil prayers for a deceased parishioner, and the following day, her funeral Mass was only for her immediate family members. The following Saturday evening, September 25, we celebrated the first parish or public Mass since mid-August with forty people. We added in additional masses across the city on that weekend, and these remained in place until November 2021, when they ceased because the overall number of attendees was very low.

The fear of the Delta variant's transmission drove these restrictions and the government mandated mask wearing for certain public events and places. Church services were recommended to use masks by the Department of Health but not mandated; our diocesan decision was to ask the congregation and clergy to wear masks at Mass. Readers and presiders could remove their masks when reading and praying the Eucharistic Prayer. The impact of Covid was seen in the prolonged return to Sunday worship during September and October of 2021. Although we offered additional Sunday masses in the Pastoral Area, none reached one hundred people during this period.

The experience in 2020 of disruption brought complications such as creating a pew booking system, policing sign-in routines, reducing lay ministry, and forbidding communion from the chalice and on the tongue—though there were individuals who insisted on this right even when it threatened other people's public safety. In 2021, we abandoned the booking system, and it made no impact as the numbers remained much lower than in 2020.

Liturgical lockdown in both 2020 and 2021 changed our parish's praying voice and our usual expectations of parish life. A new reality had dawned: no masses to attend and no priest to say them. In our two urban parishes and our one country parish, the experience was similar. Parish life came to an abrupt halt, and all our presumptions of interaction and communication had to change if we were to remain relevant and present. Our focus changed, and we worked hard to move our communications online and become accessible to parishioners. Communication, staying in touch, being seen became key drivers for all our activities.

Like others, we move quickly to develop and disseminate liturgical resources for people at home and via our website. We initiated various parishioner-based contact actions such as a Telephone Contact Tree. Contact was more straightforward in our country parish because parishioners are known to each other. In the two city parishes, the process was more time-consuming, not just because there are more parishioners, but because most people attending masses are anonymous parishioners, who have no other relationship to the parish than attending Mass.

The Pastoral Team members had to reconfigure their thinking. Before lockdown, we had operated as three discrete, though, friendly parishes. The context of our cooperation was the resignation of our bishop for inappropriate behaviour in October 2019 and the promotion of the then Cathedral Administrator to the role of Local Administrator. This seismic event in 2019 was followed, too quickly for us, by Covid. Lockdown forced us to work more as a collective, with each member working for the good of the whole. Before Covid, we had worked as a loose cooperative, sharing ideas and understanding that there would be greater unity one day. Covid accelerated this development, and the lack of a bishop meant that decisions for greater parish unity were not slowed down by episcopal inertia. The parishes finance committees decided we needed greater integration of services and funded this change. The Pastoral Team managed and delivered pastoral care across the three parishes. Doing this in a time of crisis was challenging. The team members realised that we needed to share the load by allocating tasks according to skill sets.

It became instantly apparent that the administrative processes that reflected our old thinking needed to be speedily updated. We moved our face-to-face management and administration online and invested more energy and money in cloud-based solutions. We invested in technology to remain in touch with our parishioners as they went through this rapid change experience. We also needed to learn how to communicate electronically, run our parish functions from multiple locations, and implement new communication tools simultaneously. We were implementing, training, using, and modifying at the same time. Although many businesses already operate in the cloud and are in touch with their customers and clients remotely and from diverse locations, this was a new learning experience for us.

The impact was evident in our usual work routines. It changed our information processing and decision-making from face-to-face to online meetings, email decisions, and telephone calls. These are simple examples of the depth of the institutional shift forced upon us by rapid change. The summation of this experience showed that our typical communication structures and our management processes were all pretechnological, a presumption of church life that some seem to enjoy. Our pretechnological presumptions of communication, decision-making, pastoral interaction, and management revealed how old our approach to church ministry and life really is. However, our most powerful, pre-technical communication tool, the Mass, became technological.

Losing the physical gathering of the Sunday Mass was the most significant impact of lockdown. The loss of our single most crucial parish gathering cannot be underestimated. The experience of multiple lockdowns has made the impact of this loss even more evident. The Sunday Mass is more than just a liturgical or religious gathering; it is also a social gathering and an information-sharing opportunity. It is a time to catch up and check in with people. The loss of this time meant that not only could we not perform our central, sacred duty to pray for the world, but we also could not effectively communicate with our base. The Mass gives us—as a community—a reason for being in the world. It gives the majority of parishioners a reason to be in touch and to remain in touch.

Fearing disconnection from our base, we initiated an online Sunday Mass from the cathedral presbytery. It was a tool to stay in touch with parishioners and provide them with a recognisable point of contact and ritual experience. It also provided the clergy with a tangible output that they recognised as part of their role.

As well as the online Mass, we set about developing alternative prayer forms and resources for people at home, and we began an online Sunday afternoon Liturgy of the Word. We had an undeclared fear of not communicating enough with our parishioners. The fear of being left behind in the social rush to communicate online drove our pastoral activism; it was exhausting. Staying in touch became the pastoral focus. The loss of Sunday Mass made it clear how much we rely on Mass as the community's central, physical gathering and how essential it is to parish life. Like those in the hospitality industry, our business is people. As a result of such rapid change, we made a significant investment in our operational technology throughout Covid-19 to remain in touch with our parishioners.

The most significant liturgical challenge during lockdown was not taking the Sunday Mass online; that was easy. We set up a camera in the Cathedral presbytery where three priests and one transitional deacon lived. The youngest member of the house—the deacon—was the cameraman. They organised and celebrated Sunday masses and the Easter Triduum online from their home. In a neighbouring city, two priests created a chapel in their presbytery and live-streamed masses every day, along with "conversations" and devotions. The priests wanted to do this in each instance and took the initiative.

Getting the technology in place for Mass solved one problem. Still, it didn't solve the more significant problem of communicating with parishioners who are not digitally connected. At the heart of this problem lay the challenge of getting information and prayer and liturgy resources out to all parishioners. To reach those without computers or printers, we enlisted volunteers on the Parish Telephone Tree to ask people with printers to print and deliver the newsletter and prayer resources to their neighbours.

We created home prayers and liturgies. A considerable amount of discussion went into the forms and content these should take. In collaboration with diocesan staff, we provided three prayer forms for Sundays, one for children, an entire Liturgy of Word with a table blessing and scriptural commentaries, and a third, abbreviated form of the Liturgy of the Word. We continued this pattern throughout the Triduum and Easter 2020 and in 2021. We worked on the presumption that people would do what they could and use the resources in whole or in part as they saw fit. These resources and links to virtual masses and online prayer services comprised the catalogue of the prayer resources we emailed every Friday. With Holy Week and the Paschal Triduum suspended, we developed resources for parishioners to use at home to celebrate these days, so they had more than watching others on television. We asked parishioners to place a symbol in the front window of their house, or at the gate, on each day of the Triduum to avoid losing sight of its meaning.

Lockdown disrupted our typical patterns of instruction and preparation. The catechumenate meetings went online. It was another means of staying in touch, but all other catechetical groups were suspended for the period of lockdown. These only got up and running again towards the end of 2020, and we had several false starts to sacramental processes. We paused all first communion and confirmation until 2021. We opted for a straightforward catechetical model. Before Covid, we had already moved our sacramental preparation to Sunday. We used a combination of Sunday Mass, Children's Liturgy, and a catechetical session after Mass. Together, these formed the sacramental preparation process. During July and August, we met only twice online for 10 minutes. We then decided to postpone the preparation until November 2020 because parents and children were too stressed managing online learning, home-office working, and 24/7 childcare. The preparation for the first holy communion went for four weeks throughout November 2020.

The loss of the established patterns of catechesis and worship was a challenge for our parishes' musicians and catechists. They typically prepared the liturgical rites and catechumens for Holy Week, the Paschal Triduum, and Paschal Initiation. They could not do what they expected to do and wanted to do. Even though they contributed to the production of prayer resources, there was a strong sense that while this was necessary, it was not satisfying. The halt to the usual ways of doing parish work, liturgy, and gatherings clarified how successful parish life is based on "doing things". There is an essential need for people to be active, doing things; a pastoral activism.

Pastoral activism was evident in how we went about getting online masses and prayers up and running. It was evident in the work we put into developing and implementing management systems and the time spent creating home-based liturgies. All of this was done because we could not physically gather. Because we could not physically gather, we could not communicate. As a result, we had to reassess what makes us a parish. Are we still a parish and still relevant when we cannot do the activities that make us a parish? And are we still relevant when we cannot communicate our value through our activities? It became clear that much of parish life is driven by pastoral activism. Without it, a parish is vulnerable to irrelevancy. What do we offer the contemporary person if our modern parish is driven by the parish's own need to be needed?

In May 2021, we were fortunate to celebrate the Pentecost Vigil—with limited numbers of 100— and the initiation rites with catechumens and candidates. It was an extraordinary occasion because it was also the first public Mass after the lockdown restrictions were lifted. It held not only a special solemnity of Christian initiation but also a deep sense of gratitude that we could gather again. We were acutely aware of the many places where people could not gather for worship.

Communication

Parishioners who were regularly in contact with the parish offices as a form of social communication struggled because they had lost their everyday, habitual behaviours. Realising we needed to contact as many people as possible, we introduced a Pastoral Telephone Tree. We quickly learned that our parish database was woefully outdated.

Initially, three Pastoral Team members created and coordinated the Pastoral Telephone Tree. They divided the available parish rolls between them. With groups of volunteers, they phoned everyone on the lists and updated their details as they went. The responsible team members debriefed on the contact process and updated the contacts lists every Friday morning. They also noted any special needs identified by the calling team and followed up with people identified as vulnerable. All this information was given to the parish secretary, who entered the information in the parish database. The new, revised calling list was emailed to the pastoral team members each Monday morning. They then emailed these lists to their volunteer contacts.

Initially, the Pastoral Team identified those parishioners we considered our most vulnerable. They included the elderly without family support, those with mental health issues, those who lived alone or were new to the parish, and the financially vulnerable. We phoned them first. Having identified them, we assessed their needs and stayed in contact or put them in touch with other social agencies if required.

Our most significant innovation in communication was our online newsletter, *Kotahi Ano* (Ourselves Together). Through the newsletter, we sent out information, and we gathered data to correct our database; it was a monumental task. By the end of lockdown, the circulation was 650 discrete email addresses; it is now over 800. The newsletter content changed radically from parish notices to including information on Covid-19, links to local government and national government websites, information on health and well-being, scripture reflections, reading material, and pastoral information. It also included all our worship and music resources for those at home prayer. *Kotahi Ano* became the single online newsletter for all three parishes. Begun as a PDF emailed to parishioners, it has evolved into an online, web-based newsletter. This newsletter became our flagship communication.

Because the initial newsletter was an emailed PDF, it had to be printed. This built within me the awareness that pastoral leadership includes facilitating the ability of parishioners to see a need and respond to it! Many parishioners took it upon themselves to print copies for their neighbours who either did not have access to the internet or did not have a printer. This continues today.

Back to Business

After the lockdown, we assessed what we had learned throughout the change experience. We had come face to face with ourselves as an organisation unprepared to meet this challenge. Our enfeebled, top-down decision processes slowed us down until we decided to make team members and committees responsible for rapid decision-making. We used online meetings to work through the decision-making process to meet the multiple demands.

We came face-to-face with our aged population and the lack of younger people involved in parish life. During lockdown in 2020, our key social outreach group could not operate because only four of their twenty members were under 70 years of age.[5] Suddenly all the work this group does with incredible generosity stopped. As a result, the Catholic community did not have a face in the city, and we could not directly contribute to the social services and outreach of the civic authorities. This brought into focus our need to foster the participation of younger people in social outreach activities.

Having communicated online for several weeks once we came back at the end of lockdown, it became apparent that many wanted to return to the old communication patterns and reinstate the paper newsletter, especially at the Cathedral parish. Here the resistance to change was much stronger than in the other two parishes. I think this reflects three things: first, the Cathedral parish is an older and more entrenched population that has been protected from change over the years; second, that the other two parishes were more acquainted with change and loss; and third, the nature of grief and the need for certainties to return that mark an end to the lockdown experience. The compromise created a shortened (or shorter) PDF version that people could print out at home. This version is printed for those who request it and parishioners in rest homes.

In fact, the return to business as usual after the 2020 lockdown happened quickly. For example, on my daily walks during the lockdown, I had acknowledged everyone I passed with a "hi" or "gidday", and others did the same for me. I had crossed major roads without traffic, looking neither left nor right. After lockdown, this stopped. Within a week of freedom, I passed people on the street without saying anything. The traffic flow increased, and roads filled again.

In the second main lockdown of 2021, the general attitude to social and physical distancing differed noticeably from 2020, with many more cars on the streets, more noise and less physical distancing. In September, once lockdown was lifted in our part of the country, churches remained closed for two more weeks. The impact of the 2021 lockdown on Mass attendance was very noticeably more significant than after the 2020 lockdown. From mid-September to the beginning of November, the return to worship was much slower. By comparison, our attendance count was halved. Once we were allowed to gather with up to one hundred people, attendants never reached one hundred in any city church over the first six weeks.

A New Vocabulary

Covid-19 has given us a new vocabulary, including social distancing, physical distancing, domestic bubbles, non-essential and essential workers, non-essential and essential businesses, contactless shopping, isolation, and track and trace. For parishioners and clergy alike, our new words are liturgical lockdown, virtual and online Mass, walk-up communion, drive through confessions, and spiritual communion.

For our parishes, liturgical lockdown also meant pastoral life lockdown. We had to readjust our whole concept of pastoral ministry. Liturgical lockdown brought our mediated sacramental life to a sudden halt. Since Vatican II, the liturgical lockdown is the most significant disruption to Catholic liturgical and pastoral practice. Social distancing, church closures and weeks without masses and sacraments changed the practice of religion and our concept of community. The gathered community—in every form—became the danger. Because liturgical gatherings were forbidden, we turned to the online or virtual world. We redefined our understanding of the liturgical community through virtual participation and redefined mediation as virtual, not physical.

Through forced isolation, church life and Sunday worship changed. For all, it became domestic, and for some, it became virtual. Virtual masses arose everywhere to solve the crisis of no physical gatherings. Going virtual distanced the liturgical community from its foundational physicality.

"Social distancing" brought an unintended negative psychological response, and it was soon changed to "physical distancing" when people started reporting feeling isolated and suicidal. The lockdown experience was too much for many, including parishioners, and several became very unwell.

This change in vocabulary illustrates why words matter and when using a term also has unintended consequences. The context of rapid social change meant that we had to find new words to describe old things. As the human impacts of Covid became more noticeable, we began to see that community is a double-edged reality. It is an essential driver of human well-being and part of the fabric of church life and social life, and it is the source of Covid infections. Distance brought safety, and community brought threat, so Sunday worship was restricted. The loss of community and the danger of physical community is a crucial part of the story of Covid-19 and liturgical lockdown.

We produced vast amounts of worship material worldwide, and the number of virtual masses increased enormously. Parishes, clergy and dioceses embraced social and physical distancing. Priests admitted being pleased with more attendees online than they usually had. Physical and social isolation was embraced as the resurgent, liturgical form.

While social and physical isolation dug deeper for many, the church reinvented itself. It created a parallel world where physical presence and community were irrelevant. The central theological tenents of gathering and community essential to the Eucharist were replaced with individual prayer forms that aped community. Practices like "spiritual communion" became normative, and the falsehood that those watching an online Mass were actually participating in it was never challenged.

The justification for these responses is explored throughout the following sections.

---

[1] The Innovator's Dilemma, 323.

[2] The Innovator's Dilemma, 323.

[3] The Innovator's Dilemma, XVII.

[4] The Innovator's Dilemma, 323.

[5] Those 70 years and over were advised under government guidelines not to leave their homes except for recreational walks.

A Disrupted and Innovated Laity

Christensen was not just referring to successful innovations that made good products even better, more accessible, or easier to use. He drew attention to the type of innovation that removes the historical hegemony of a single group of product users. By removing exclusive access to a product or service through providing a replacement or similar service or product to a broader, more diverse audience, innovation disrupts established elites and their control over the product or service. The service or product becomes democratised and achieves a new group of consumers. An example of this is the personal computer. Personal computers have made computing available to the masses and innovated computing technology, social contact, and information availability through easier access and cheaper ownership.

The disruption to the liturgical and pastoral experience brought significant innovation to the prayer forms of the laity. As the Pastoral Team transferred its energy from face-to-face encounters to online encounters and offered online worship, products, and services to support parishioners, we did this using sustaining technologies. At the behest of our parishioners who wanted access to "church" even when it was not physically possible, we transferred our labour, worship, presence, products, and services to the digital world

Liturgical Lockdown

Covid-19 disrupted the liturgical experience and expectations of the laity and innovated the domestic lay church through innovating worship patterns and pastoral expectations. Covid gave the domestic setting the choice to participate in established prayer forms or create new ones. Restrictions on physical gatherings forced New Zealand Catholics to pray and worship at home, alone, and in family groups. While many joined virtual worship opportunities, a significant number did not. These people developed their own home or domestic prayer forms. Many used the prayer resources we offered online. This section focuses mainly on the domestic world and the laity's response to the liturgical and pastoral lockdown.

Survey Results

In two surveys in 2021 at the end of the August lockdown, I asked for feedback from the laity on their experience of virtual liturgy, prayer during the lockdown and pastoral interaction.[1] Survey One was parish-based, and Survey Two went nationally. I asked similar questions in both surveys, and each survey contained four control questions.

Most respondents characterised the virtual mass as "comforting" in each survey. However, their written responses suggest that "comforting" is less than desirable.

Table One

Survey Response	Parish Responses	National Responses
Comforting	16.22%	25.29%
Very good	14.86%	10.34%
Better than nothing	13.51%	8.05%
Odd	10.81%	9.20%
Challenging	9.46%	3.45%
Uncomfortable	9.46%	2.30%
A little strange	9.46%	9.20%
Excellent	8.11%	17.24%
Positive	8.11%	14.94%

Survey Written Responses:2

Watching priests praying and receiving communion not spiritually uplifting: No participation.

Able to flick between Masses and choose the one with the best optics! Not prayerful.

"Online Mass" is fundamentally not the Mass – when I "attend" over a computer screen, I am not present to the mystery being celebrated, and Jesus has not come to me in the flesh. However, I am still glad to have watched many online Masses from around the world, thus giving me exposure to different rites and forms of Mass that I wouldn't have encountered at my regular parish church.

It was sterile.

Not community, not communion, no Communion.

It's difficult to create transcendence by looking at a screen.

Initially, it was comforting as we gathered as a religious community. But it was not as satisfying as being present at parish Eucharist, and toward the end of lockdown, I really didn't want to participate anymore online.

I experienced a special closeness to the Paschal Mystery – just myself and Jesus in the hands of the priest.

No community, no Eucharist, clerical, could read/reflect on the Word myself.

Seeing an exclusively male, clerical depiction of "the source and summit" of our relationship with God is very limiting.

The priest alone is not good for the church.

I loved the Mass in my own home as I live on my own in a Retirement Village.

I viewed the liturgy of the word and sermon. Never the liturgy of the eucharist. I had no interest in watching a priest "picnic at the top of the hill in full view" while the rest of us went without.

I was led to an objective re-think of the part Mass takes in my prayer life.

The main thing I missed was the actual reception of communion and seeing people face to face, but I enjoyed the variety of online masses.

I have several great online masses to go to and use them often.

Inappropriate form of the Eucharist.

Some were very formal, but others more relaxed.

Not the real presence. Incomplete.

It connected me with the worshipping Church.

It was difficult with many distractions happening at home, or I was with my father, who was dying in hospital (Level 4).

It was good to be with other parishioners in praying together and enjoyed the homilies each day.

It was interesting to see the likenesses and differences from NZ practice.

At many of the online Masses, the experience was uncomfortable. Low-quality camera, poor sound and, more often than not, the vestments, altar candles and liturgical vessels were shoddy.

In each survey, respondents were asked the following question: "How did you pray during Covid-Lockdown? Did you use other forms of prayer?". They were asked to rate the statements in Table Two below according to their personal practice during the lockdown. Respondents were asked to use one of the following responses: "I mostly did this", "I often did this", "I sometimes did this", or "I never did this". Table Two highlights the difference between "I mostly did this" and "I never did this".[3]

Table Two

Survey One (Parish)	I mostly did this	I never did this
I said my own prayers	50%	6%
I said my own form of Mass at home	*0.5*	*96.*
I didn't bother with Sunday Mass or prayers	0.5	76. 9
I prayed family prayers	14	52.
I read the scriptures each day	*45*	*20*
I prayed the Rosary each day	*19*	*39*
I meditated	36	22
I used Lectio Divina	17	46
I used another form of prayer.	24	43
Survey Two (National)	**I mostly did this**	**I never did this**
I joined an online prayer group	6	70.
I said my own form of Mass at home	*3.*	*95.*
I used an online Sunday Liturgy of Word	23	52.
I prayed the Rosary each day	*24*	*53*
I read the Scriptures each day	*26*	*33*
I created my own Sunday worship	10	60
I didn't bother with Sunday Mass or prayers	*2*	*88*

These responses show that most respondents used their own prayer forms and read the daily scriptures during the lockdown. The daily scriptures outranked praying the Rosary in each survey by a small margin. The response "I never did this" is informative of individual priorities. In each survey, the majority wanted some form of the Sunday Mass, but only a tiny percentage said their own home Mass and a similarly small percentage didn't bother with Sunday Mass or prayers at all. The trend is clear that most respondents could continue their prayer life during the lockdown. Although a majority used an online or virtual mass, the majority did not access an online liturgy of Word.

I think this shows the strength of the domestic church to care for itself, as the majority of respondents observed Sunday in some way. The most used form of non-eucharistic prayer was daily scripture reading. Most people operated independently, and a small but consistent group celebrated a form of home eucharistic.

While most online groups focussed on masses, some focussed on liturgies of the Word, with sharing on Sundays. The survey reflects a lower use of this format than for virtual masses because fewer options for online Liturgy of the Word or prayer times were available.

Our parish group offered an online Liturgy of the Word on Sundays and an online Liturgy of the Hours prayer time during the week. The virtual Liturgy of the Word was interactive in that participants took various parts, some reading and others singing. While groups were consistent in their numbers, these were not high. Once the restrictions were lifted, these two online activities disappeared within six weeks.

Liturgical Lockdown

Respondents were asked to identify the most significant impact of Covid lockdown 2020 on them. From the mainly female, predominantly over 60-year age group, a pattern emerged, the loss of daily routines. Their most significant loss was the Mass, for two contrasting reasons.

For Group A, theirs was the loss of community, but for Group B, it was the loss of holy communion. For each group, the Mass is a relational experience but not in the same way or with the same focus. The distinction between groups A and B is the Mass's role in sustaining their personal motivations. Group A I would typify as those who *gather at the Mass for community,* and Group B as those who *gather at Mass for holy communion.*

Group A's primary relationship is to their parish community and community of friendships, and the Mass is their meeting point. This group gathers *at the Mass* because the Mass forms a primary reason for their gathering, but the Mass is not just a social function; it is also a spiritual experience. For this group, the Mass functions primarily as the place of the religious or church community. Its loss as a regular feature in the week also meant the loss of habitual, social community and friendships.

While the loss of the Mass was the direct experience, the indirect loss of community and friendship was more significant. Although this group also experienced the loss of holy communion, it was not their direct experience because their attendance at Mass is not driven primarily or solely by the reception of communion. The majority of respondents in this group described the online or virtual Mass as "better than nothing". However, most of them quickly grew tired of it and ceased using it.

Group B I have characterised as those who *gather for holy communion at Mass.* Their primary focus in attending Mass is to receive holy communion and only secondarily to gather with the community. The community does not draw this group into worship or keep them there. The characteristic motives for this groups' attendance at Mass are the reception of Holy Communion and their own individual prayer. Thus, members of this group missed Mass and communion, but they did not miss the community at Mass to the same extent.

Because the community of the Mass does not play a central role in their social system, their attendance at it and their primary motivation for attendance is the personal, private quality of the experience. For this Group, Mass is a private activity that relies on an internalised, individual relationship to the Eucharist expressed in their individual reception of Holy Communion. Because they could not receive Holy Communion, they experienced the indirect loss more acutely than the direct loss.

Group B members showed higher use of virtual masses over a more extended period and a higher acceptance of the notion and practice of spiritual communion. They took greater comfort in seeing the Mass "said" and hearing the priest say it.

The critical differentiator between these groups is the role of community in worship and parish. For both, the Mass is a vehicle for something more personal and indirect. This suggests that the value given to "the Mass" is reliant on, or defined by, other priorities.

Members of each group come from what Christensen would describe as the "mainstream customers" (98% of respondents who answered these questions self-identified as regular Sunday Mass attendees, and 50% identified as daily weekday Mass attendees).

Despite the loss of community, parish, Mass, and holy communion, 70% of all respondents agreed that the lockdown was the right action to take, and they agreed with the closure of churches. Sixty per cent of all respondents agreed that public safety comes before religious activity. The lockdown offered 30% of respondents the opportunity to rethink their lifestyles.

Sixty per cent of those who went online for Mass reported that Mass was for them primarily either a spiritual exercise or a personal need. The majority of respondents showed a clear preference for masses online and did not see the absence of the laity as an impediment.

Less than 50% of respondents agreed that their attendance as laity at Mass was very important or even essential. This finding is fascinating. It could suggest that the Mass—whether for communion or community—is still primarily the priest's action, and attending laity have other reasons for being there. It could suggest that attendance is driven by other motivations that are deeper and more authentic than community or communion. It also suggests a transactional approach to liturgy.

The notion of "spiritual communion" equally attracted and repulsed respondents. Their response aligned with their approach to Mass as either a community or a personal experience. The majority of those who surfed the internet for virtual masses—and who missed communion—saw spiritual communion as a consolation.

Other Forms of Worship

Those who did not find the virtual masses helpful sometimes turned to other forms of prayer. Several parishioners told me they watched one or two virtual masses and then gave up on them because, in the words of one, "they were not real". Some parishioners reported joining other Zoom and Skype prayer groups to see others and share prayers and scripture reflections. Seeing other people became an essential element of the virtual prayer times during the experience of social and physical isolation. Alternative forms of worship and prayer democratised liturgy through being accessible to all. These "democratised" forms of worship also used a democratised form of leadership, where everyone and anyone could lead. However, once restrictions were lifted, the desire for lay-led liturgy and different forms of prayer remained, but the practice did not. Even these democratic and flexible prayer forms disappeared.

In 2020 the domestic lay scene saw other forms of liturgical or worship innovation in what came to be called family or individual "liturgical bubbles". The liturgical bubble reflected the wider domestic bubbles we were asked to remain in as a means of limiting the effects of infection. The personal, domestic bubble was true for clergy and laity. In the prayer bubble, the biblical maxim: "Where two or three are gathered in my name I am there in their midst" (Matthew, 18: 20) became the maxim of prayer, socialisation, and entertainment. Choice and innovation also included replacing established forms and places of prayer and worship with new domestic and improvised ones.

In 2020, "bubble prayers" came in two forms, short and long. The short forms were written for churchgoers who are less accustomed to church language and ritual and focussed on a single action or idea. Longer forms were adaptations of formal practices from the Easter Triduum or Sundays during 2020. Both forms had a shared meal and relied on the tradition of worship, reaching back to the earliest tradition of Christian household prayer, like the Agape. These resources were also offered in a children's format with language and activities appropriate for school-aged children. These prayer forms were created to enable the domestic church to pray as part of the universal church. In our context, prayers were made available in multiple languages.

The structure of the gathering and prayer took various forms, depending on the group praying. Parents with young children sought to open the scriptures to them in ways the children could appreciate. Inevitably, the prayer forms we offered to parishioners were further modified by them. Individual circumstances informed and shaped the level, style, and structure of the prayers that individuals and families used.

Some parents reported adapting these resources even more for very young children. Most parents lead simple, activity-based, or nature-based worship. With older children and teenagers, family worship forms included discussions and self-written prayers in addition to "liturgical meals" or "lay eucharist". While those who used "liturgical meals" or "lay-eucharist" found it more authentic than watching a priest say Mass online, they did not want to call this experience the Eucharist because it was not a community experience of ministry and worship.

Some families and individuals used a "liturgical meal" with scripture readings and the offering of a glass of wine and a piece of bread—that they shared—with song. These liturgical meals that started as a substitute for the Sunday Eucharist became, for some, their "lay eucharist".

The meal nearly always included the offering of bread and a glass of wine, intending to remember the night of the Last Supper, but not necessarily to replace the Mass. Others combined a liturgical meal with an actual Sunday meal, reimaging the Early Church's worship patterns.

Whether they saw their meal as a substitute for the Mass or equal to the Mass remains unclear. The experience opened a conversation concerning the nature of ministry, worship, and Eucharist, not only in a time of crisis but in ordinary times too. It became a conversation about the nature of mediated sacraments, asking if—the priest mediator cannot be present—the lay-form is equally good, if not currently valid?

While many spoke of their sense of authentic worship at home through innovation, most wanted to return to Sunday worship. However, this was tempered by a greater expectation of change and innovation. Though sustained by "their" domestic church, they also expressed their concern at the formal liturgical life of the parish. They had recognised a gap between the formal liturgical life of the parish and the liturgical life they had created in their own homes.[4]

They spoke of the need to incorporate the home experience in the parish worship once we returned. In one church, we acknowledged this by adding an additional Mass with a simplified rite and rearranging the seating into family groups. We continued this from 2020 until the August lockdown in 2021.

The experience of home worship does not appear to have diminished the overall desire for community and Sunday worship, but it has reshaped the expectation of what the Sunday Mass should be like and how it should function as an inclusive action. I think this is a result of how families worshipped during the lockdown.

For many people, this period was transformative because worship was not transactional. The lockdown experience of prayer engendered a heightened sense of community, even when the community was their household. Those who responded to surveys and in conversations reported a naturally heightened desire for physical, communal gatherings.

Liturgical Lockdown

As a result of this experience, many respondents expect more participation in Sunday liturgy than before lockdown. Those who preferred virtual worship were content to continue with the online form. Here, we begin to see a distinction between a transformative and a transactional liturgical imperative.

A Disrupted and Innovated Priesthood

The clergy's world was disrupted during the lockdown, and the virtual masses gave us a privileged view into their domestic lives. We saw priests and bishops sitting at their dining tables, in their living rooms and offices and in empty churches offering their virtual Mass and devotions. This gave us a glimpse into the deeper thinking regarding clerical ministry and life in an institution trained for a pre-Covid world. [5]

This chapter focuses on the impact of liturgical lockdown on the clergy and their response to parish ministry and liturgy loss. It relies on a survey that was answered by priests from five of New Zealand's six dioceses in June 2021. The survey respondents ranged from 25 to over 80 years of age, of whom the majority were diocesan priests. The survey focussed on the first lockdown from the end of March to the middle of May 2020.

This survey, together with professional conversations, one focus group, and a large variety of internationally published material on the clergy response to Covid and liturgical lockdown, underpin this chapter's comments and analysis. [6] Clergy and their motivations are complex and can be too quickly oversimplified, which is the risk I run here. Let me be very clear in what follows: I am not questioning at any point the efficacy of the Mass when celebrated under any form permitted by the liturgical books. Instead, I am asking the reader to consider the culture of spirituality, priesthood, authority, and more that we apply to the Mass as a possession.

Liturgical Lockdown

Where priests lived together in presbyteries, their rationale was slightly different. While many priests defaulted to virtual Mass from their domestic world, others did not. I chose to share the deprivation of the parishioners as one-with-them and prayed with them each Sunday. Another priest colleague told me, "It's weird answering myself back; it's just ritualism", and so he discontinued his private Mass. Many priests who said Mass on their own, with or without a live-streamed audience, felt more connected to their raison d'être for being a priest. Some experienced peer pressure to conform and some used the Mass to express their shared priesthood. Some did what they always did and started the day with Mass followed by muesli. To be fair, priests were encouraged by Vatican and episcopal directives to celebrate Mass alone on weekdays and Sundays, during Holy Week, and during the Paschal Triduum (*Decree In Time of Covid-19*, Vatican 19 March 2020) to which we will come.

Why The Virtual Sunday Mass?

The first survey question asked respondents if they had celebrated or concelebrated Sunday Mass during the Covid lockdown in 2020 and 79.69% replied that they had, 20% did not. The 20% who did not celebrate Sunday Mass at all during the lockdown gave their reasons for their decisions:

> There were sufficient online Masses being offered.
>
> I did not think it appropriate to celebrate Eucharist without the people. Instead, my colleague and I celebrated a liturgy of the Word together.
>
> Lockdown.
>
> I attended Mass. I thought we should put our energy into the Word of God.

I am semi-retired.

I'm retired and not committed to any Sunday Mass.

The people are essential.

The people couldn't, so I did not. I am a priest for and with the people. Celebrating Mass without the community seemed wrong.

Of those who celebrated Sunday Mass, 55.10% celebrated offline because of their age or unfamiliarity with the technology, and the remaining 44.9% celebrated an online or virtual Mass. Of the 44.9% who celebrated a virtual Mass, 24% were members of a "concelebrant" group, and almost 20% of the 44.9% celebrated alone. A total of 36% of this group used an online platform for their Sunday Mass. Still, only 12% of them included some form of viewer participation; this was done predominantly by priests celebrating alone, with their parishioners on Zoom, sharing ritual functions like readings, prayer and singing. Of those who used technology for Sunday Mass, 22.2% used Zoom, 15.56% used YouTube, and 2.2% used Microsoft Teams.

The priests who included viewer participation in their virtual masses mainly used Zoom because it was free, easy to install or download and could handle most groups. It also provided a breakout room facility that more sophisticated users used for scripture sharing. Virtual participation was always pre-arranged, and viewers led the readings, prayers, music, and songs. Those who used YouTube could not include this level of participation because their masses were "view only".

While 77% of respondents used the Mass as part of their regular prayer regime throughout lockdown, a larger number (83.88%) used the Divine Office, making it the main form of personal prayer used by the clergy during the lockdown.

Only 3.33% led an online Liturgy of the Word for their parish, while 20% participated in one. The majority (60%) did not use or engage in other online prayer opportunities beyond their own masses. No respondents led or participated in an online scripture study group. However, 10% led an online scripture reflection group, and 13% participated in one. The Mass was clearly central to the prayer life of clerics during the lockdown.

In order to find out why most respondents celebrated Mass without the laity's physical presence and active participation, it was necessary to ask more questions to ascertain if this response was normative or exceptional. Question One was linked to four control questions later in the survey. The control questions were designed to probe deeper into their understanding of the liturgy *vis-a-vis* the use of virtual masses, the presence and participation of laity and fundamental theological concepts of the liturgy. Respondents were forced to reply to the control questions using one of the following responses:

> Most important for me
> Very important for me
> Important for me
> Often important for me
> Least important for me

The first control question asked: "When you think about the Sunday Mass, how would you rank the following options?

> Mass is a dialogue between God and humankind: 53.13%
> Mass is the gathering of the community: 37.50%
> Mass is the exercise of the priesthood: 9.38%
> Mass is a personal spiritual exercise: 0.00%
> Mass is the forgiveness of sins: 0.00%

The second question asked respondents to rank the following statements from *Sacrosanctum Concilium*:

> The Mass is the source and summit: 67.74%
> The Mass is an exercise of the priestly office of Christ: 18.75%
> The Mass is the gathering of the community: 12.50%
> The Mass is the activity of the Church: 3.13%
> The Mass is the foretaste of heaven: 0.0%

Question three asked respondents to consider the nature of the congregation's physical presence for the Sunday Mass:

> Physical presence is absolutely essential: 46.88%
> Physical presence is generally essential but not absolutely essential: 40.63%
> Physical presence is good but not essential: 9.38%
> Physical presence is not always essential and not always necessary: 3.13%
> Physical presence is not essential and not necessary: 0.0%

Question four asked respondents to rank the active participation of the congregation in the Sunday Mass:

> Active participation is absolutely essential: 68.75%
> Active participation is generally essential but not absolutely essential: 18.75%
> Active participation is good to have but not absolutely essential: 6.25%
> Active participation is good but not essential: 3.13%
> Active participation is not always essential and not always necessary: 0.00%

Liturgical Lockdown

> Active participation is not essential and not
> necessary: 3.13%

When we rank their majority responses from highest to lowest, we have a snapshot of the respondent's theological thinking:

> The active participation by the laity is
> absolutely essential in Mass: 68.75%
> The Mass is the source and summit: 67.74%
> The Mass is a dialogue between God and
> humankind: 53.13%
> The physical presence of the laity is
> absolutely essential for Mass: 46.88%

Active participation of the laity at 68.75% and 67.74% support for the Mass as "source and summit" support *Sacrosanctum Concilium*'s theology of the Mass. Liturgy as a "dialogue between God and humankind" is just over 50%, but less than 50% of respondents hold that the laity's physical presence at Mass is essential. We have to read the answers in light of the baseline knowledge that all who responded to these questions also celebrated Mass each Sunday of lockdown without the laity's presence and comprise the majority of respondents at 79.69%. There is a discrepancy between holding a theology about the liturgy and enacting a liturgical praxis that reflects it. This is a discrepancy between conceptual theology and liturgical theological praxis.

The discrepancy begins to appear when one contrasts that 79.69% of all respondents celebrated a Sunday Mass online or privately during the lockdown without the active presence or participation of the laity despite 46.88% of those respondents agreeing that the physical presence of the laity at Sunday Mass is absolutely essential. And 68.75% of 79.69% of respondents agreed that the active participation of the laity at Sunday Mass is absolutely essential. Still, only 36% of them offered any form of lay participation in online worship.

The discrepancy between action and thinking is further explained by looking at those who did not answer in the majority and calculating their answers. Doing this, we see another pattern emerging:

The physical presence of the laity at Sunday Mass (total 53.14%):

> Physical presence is generally essential but not absolutely essential: 40.63%
> Physical presence is good but not essential: 9.38%
> Physical presence is not always essential and not always necessary: 3.13%
> Physical presence is not essential and not necessary: 0.0%

Active participation of the laity in the Sunday Mass (total 31.26%):

> Active participation is generally essential but not absolutely essential: 18.75%
> Active participation is good to have but not absolutely essential: 6.25%
> Active participation is good but not essential: 3.13%
> Active participation is not always essential and not always necessary: 0.00%
> Active participation is not essential and not necessary: 3.13%

The more significant answer concerns the laity's physical presence at Sunday Mass. A total of 53.14% of all respondents (79.69%) who celebrated masses on Sunday agreed that the laity's physical presence at Sunday Mass *is less than absolutely essential.* By comparison, fewer respondents (31.26%) agreed that the active participation of the laity at Sunday Mass is *less than absolutely essential.* The more influential group is those who do not see the laity's physical presence at Mass as absolutely essential, suggesting that what drives down lay presence at the Mass—in the eyes of priests—is the non-essential nature of their presence. It also suggests that active participation and physical presence are not considered equivalent in the thinking of the majority of respondents. When one puts the results together, most of those who celebrated Mass on Sundays during lockdown did so without either the active presence or the active participation of the laity because their presence and participation were not essential.

Between Theology and Practice

We have a clear, but not a unanimous, understanding of the Mass as a central action of the cleric. But is this inconsistency just a matter of language? Is it reasonable to suggest an equivalent relationship between active participation and liturgical presence? Suppose these terms are not related, equivalent or dependent on each other. In that case, the higher percentage of those agreeing with the concept of active participation is probably explained by this phrase's long-standing use in theological literature and discourse. In contrast, the unfamiliarity of "liturgical presence" may explain its lower rating.

Given that words mean different things to different people, there is always room for interpretation. Thus, is it reasonable to presume that all clergy are familiar with *Sacrosanctum Concilium*'s principle of liturgical participation as a theological concept but not with the concept of liturgical presence? I think this is possible. If active participation is more widely known and understood than liturgical presence, why is this theological concept not translated into liturgical action? Here is a significant discrepancy between what is understood theologically and what is done liturgically. It is a discrepancy between the *theology of the liturgy* and the *liturgical praxis of that theology.* It is illustrative of an "accepted theology" not being a practised theology.

It seems possible—at least theoretical—for clergy to hold that active liturgical participation is a central principle of the liturgy without needing, at the same time, to make it a central principle of liturgical practice. There appears to be a breakdown between principle and its incarnation in action. The same is true of liturgical presence. The breakdown between "knowing" and "doing" is a breakdown between the ideal and the actual. Put another way: what the clergy say about the laity's presence and participation in the liturgy is not matched by their actions. The inconsistency exposes fundamental clerical presumptions of the Mass, their role in it and their relationship to the lay members of the Church as participants of it.

The discrepancy between saying Mass without a congregation on the one hand, and affirming lay participation and presence at Mass on the other, illustrates not only the disconnect between a *theology of the liturgy* and a *theological praxis in the liturgy* but also a disconnect between the roles of presider and laity as presences of Christ in the liturgical act. This discrepancy is illustrative of a non-relational understanding of liturgical presence and participation. Thus, one cannot assume that the laity's liturgical participation and active participation in the liturgy are the driving theological principles of clerical liturgical practice. This would explain why the driving theological idea among respondents concerning the Mass was not the laity's participation or presence but their own.

Liturgical Lockdown

This break suggests a qualitative difference between the clergy's presence and activity, and the laity's presence and activity in the liturgy are normative for clerics. It suggests that in the clerical theological worldview, liturgical presence and liturgical participation by the laity do not have to be either physical, or participatory. The usual relationality of physicality, activity, participation, and presence that would exist at a birthday party or dinner is not considered when it comes to the ritual meal of the Eucharist. This must be because liturgical presence and participation rely on a unique concept of relationality that is not essentially immediate, physical, or proximate. Because this "unique" notion of relationality is not relational in any sense approaching common sense, it must be "theological" and therefore capable of speaking about full, conscious, and active participation without inferring that any of this is physical, active, participatory and proximate.

Have we found the clergy's new "normal" for worship in a time of the pandemic, or have we just seen the already existing "default position"? I suspect we have merely seen the already existing default position in operation. However, we need to balance this conclusion by considering those priests who would not typically have celebrated Mass without a physically present, lay community who then celebrated a private or online Mass. We must also allow for those priests and bishops who felt forced into the virtual form of Mass, either through a sense of offering consolation or through the expectation to perform. Equally, we must not forget the majority of the laity's desire to have priests "say Mass" in the virtual environment and the anger of some of them at priests who chose not to. The relational disconnect between the laity's active participation and physical presence at the liturgy is "theologically true", not just for most clerics but also for most of the laity.

Some will argue that the laity was impeded from attending, not just unavailable or just "not there", and that this accounts for the situation. I am not so sure. The fact the laity were impeded from attending should have been more substantial grounds for not celebrating masses because the Body of Christ was impeded from gathering. Because this was not the case, I think we have seen the default or normative position and not an exceptional response. My conclusion is further supported by the fact the general clerical behaviour did not change throughout the lockdown experience because the laity's physical presence and active participation at Mass is not the driving liturgical principle for the clergy. If it was, then more priests would not have celebrated Mass without the presence of the laity as a presence of Christ and members of the Body of Christ.

Pastoral Impacts for Clergy

Respondents were asked to identify the most significant disruption to their ministry during the lockdown. Answers grouped around (1) not being able to physically engage with parishioners in pastoral ministry, (2) confinement and lack of general social contact, and (3) lack of sacramental ministry (see Appendix Two). As non-essential workers, priests were forbidden to enter hospitals, aged-care facilities, and private homes unless they were designated, essential workers. Because the overwhelming majority were classified as non-essential workers, they were expected to remain at home. The expectation was even more vital for those over 70 years of age. Being designated by the government as "non-essential workers", clergy could not leave their houses or properties for work-related activities. This included entering their church and saying masses. Although most respondents (58 %) disagreed with this designation, a significant minority (42%) agreed. Nonetheless, 87% of respondents agreed that closing all churches and ceasing public worship at level four was the correct decision.

Although most respondents (53.33%) stated that their pastoral work was vital, they did not communicate more with their parishioners during the lockdown. Those who could access a digital platform used it almost exclusively for virtual masses and for staying in touch with friends and family. Asked if their communication with parishioners during lockdown was "more, less or about the same as before lockdown", 41% indicated they communicated about the same as before lockdown, 36% communicated more during the lockdown, and 23% communicated less than before lockdown.

The clergy's response to the communications question compared with the responses in the two surveys of laypeople shows a discrepancy between what each group considers communication. The lay respondents considered the clergy's efforts at communication were less than expected throughout lockdown. The notion of communication is probably understood differently by clergy and parishioners and thus their expectations. For the majority of the clergy, communication meant saying Mass online and, for some, privately. An example of this came in a letter from a priest colleague. He wrote: "I am saying Mass for the intentions of the parish and saving souls". He was not in touch with his parishioners via the internet or telephone throughout the 2020 lockdown because he was 'in touch with them through the Holy Sacrifice of the Mass and the spiritual communion.' For some respondents, but not a majority, the telephone was the only pastoral aid they used. For lay respondents, communication included online information and personal phone calls.

Another pastoral impact was their confinement to their houses. For the first time in the lives of many priests, they were prevented from working and literally could not open the church. The day could not start with Mass and carry on in and around the parish office and church. The motivation to "keep the shop open and the lights on" was strong for many. It was vital for them to be seen as participants in the pandemic response and show that the Church is necessary and active, a place of consolation, advice, well-being, and charity, even when religious gatherings were considered health risks and public gatherings were forbidden.

For many, being excluded from leading funerals was disheartening. For one colleague in a neighbouring parish, it meant standing at the back of the hearse, and sprinkling holy water on the casket, as the hearse stopped momentarily at the Church. My own experience of presiding at funerals at Level Four was gut-wrenching because families were required to bury or cremate their dead within 24 hours of death, and funerals were restricted to five people, physically distanced with others looking on via Zoom. The layering of grief meant that even the most straightforward decisions were tiring and brought more grief. Grief lay like a film of dust over an object or an ash cloud after an eruption. Much of this will resurface later as the post-traumatic impact of Covid-19 emerges. When funerals with ten participants were permitted, it was marginally better. But this was much less than what a person, or a family, wanted and needed at a time of grief and loss.

Confinement bred other forms of sacramental activism. In the United States, we saw the "drive-in Mass", the "drive-through confessional", and "drive-up communion". In the Philippines, we saw churches of empty pews adorned with pictures of parishioners who could not attend. Although these responses reflect their base cultures of fast-food, commodity-entertainment and popular religion, they reached a new low of liturgical McDonaldisation to console priests and make them feel wanted and sustain commodity-focussed customers product-based religiosity. Although these and other actions were probably well-intentioned, they relied on a thoroughly misguided pastoral-liturgical theology that sees liturgy as something to be done irrespective of circumstance. In both instances, the need to "do something" and the priest's need to communicate were dominant. Both examples illustrate a further commodification, creating products believers could consume at home or while driving through the carpark.

Sadly, in New Zealand, we were not immune from sacramental activism and the cheap, fast-food effect. One priest in Auckland advertised "walk-up communion". The deceit began with asking parishioners to park their cars on the surrounding streets so that authorities would not know there was a mass gathering. The priest, who had been live-streaming celebrations of the 1962 extraordinary rite, proposed that people could listen to the Mass in their parked cars and spiritually prepare themselves for communion. Then, they could make their way to the communion drive-through, where he would give them holy communion at the appropriate time. If he did not know or recognise them, individuals would have to answer questions about their catholicity before receiving communion. This approach reduced the Sacred Liturgy to one element, communion, and turned it into a commodity. This response directly results from the priest's lack of understanding of the foundational difference between the 1962 and 1970 Roman Missals.

When asked to reflect on the experience of liturgical disruption of 2020 and 2021 and what the Church can learn from this for the future, responses coalesced around two concerns: first, being available and present; and second, the use and impact of technology, including the skills to use it well for online worship. These two are related insofar that the concern is to be active and available in person and online. The responses show a need for a theology of digital media when used in worship (see Appendix Three), which will be more fully addressed in Part Three.

When asked to respond to the question "*What do you think will be the longest-lasting impact of level four's liturgical disruption on the parish life*?", respondents offer two key insights: first, that the lockdown had strengthened the already growing trend of non-Mass attendance and that this would contribute to ongoing decline in parish numbers and parishes; and second, that virtual Mass has contributed to the growing number of non-attendees at Sunday Mass (see Appendix Four). The longer-term impact on expectations of worship's accessibility is already seen in the approach to funerals, where the demand for live streaming has become an "ordinary" expectation. Family members "zooming" from across the globe to deliver a tribute, poem, or reading is not unusual. Often parishioners will choose the venue for the funeral service—church or funeral home—based on the Wi-Fi connectivity.

Respondents acknowledged the unresolved relationship between the need for technology in worship and the impact of digital worship on the communitarian effect of worship. Because this is not resolved, some respondents suggested the need for a theology of technology because digital worship—in the form of virtual masses, online exposition, and online prayer forms—is no longer a fringe activity. Instead, through Covid-19, it has entered the mainstream of Catholic liturgy. The unintended consequence of technology in worship is the technologization of liturgy that changes the concept of what liturgy is supposed to do and how we participate. It raises the question as to whether all worship can rightly be called liturgy in the sense of leitourgia.

---

[1] The two surveys were conducted in 2021, the first at the parish level and the second nationally. The questions were identical. IP addresses were checked to ensure that the same person had not answered twiceSurvey One, 74 respondents and Survey Two, 87. 161 respondents in total.

2 Responses are given verbatim from the surveys and have not been corrected.

3 In Table Two the percentages are given in for each statement. The statements in italics are the controls statements used in each survey.

4 Survey and interviews, Our Lady of Lourdes and the Cathedral parishes, November 2020.

5 Clergy includes priest and bishops. I refer to priests in the main because they were the majority respondents to the survey.

6 Liturgy During Lockdown and Beyond. Clergy and Level Four Liturgical Disruption during 2020. Created 17 May 2021. The respondents were from five New Zealand dioceses and ranged in age from 25 to over 80 years of age.

Covid Impacts on Priesthood

Priesthood is both an individual ministry and a shared persona. The impact of Covid on the practice priesthood has been its curtailment of ritualised pastoral and liturgical activity. I would like to offer three observations on the liturgical and pastoral solutions used by the clergy during the simultaneous experience of the liturgical, pastoral, and social lockdown. The first is the practice of communicating through ritualised behaviour, of which the Mass and the sacraments are the primary means. The second is to express priesthood in pastoral activities, and the third is to communicate and socially interact with other people.

Priests are ritualised men trained to think, respond, pray, and communicate in ritualised patterns. From the *Ubi et Orbi* to "I'll pray for you", ritualised communication forms frame the distinction between the priest—communicator—and the layperson—communicated-to—through applied institutional linguistic forms. For example, the statement "I'll pray for you" tell us who the prayer is and who the prayed-for is. This statement may be the transition from one topic or conversation to another or from one person to another. Similarly, the ministration of the sacramental rites and sacramentals—such as funerals—are institutional forms of communication used by priests. These ritualised communication forms include and exclude people depending on their knowledge and familiarity with them. Priests are highly skilled at communicating their emotions, agreement, or disagreement through the medium of rituals; rituals in the hands of a priest are never neutral!

Training in ritualised relating is the work of the seminary. Seminary training is constructed to institutionalise men and conform them to the institutionalised thinking and acting of the organisation—diocese, religious order, or congregation—they are joining. Seminary formation uses ritual behaviours to instil the group's common behaviours into the individual. Ritualisation includes the expectations of attending shared prayers, meals and daily Mass. Ritual participation legitimates living in the seminary, and participating in legitimated prayer forms is a central part of the process of "becoming" a priest. Behaviour modification through ritualisation continues throughout the training process. It ensures that an individual's thinking and actions conform to the organisation's self-understanding so the institution can be assured that the individual will comply with the organisational expectations.

Powerful behaviour modifiers are at work throughout seminary training. A seminarian must first show he fits the group, which he generally does by displaying ritualised behaviours to be ordained. Ritual behaviours are infused with divine acceptance and the threat of ecclesial expulsion. Keeping these behaviours is critical to the seminarian's acceptance and ensures his progression through the system to ordination. A seminarian's greatest vulnerability is the need for his call to the vocation of the priesthood to be legitimated by an external, authorising hierarch.

Over time, the seminarian's personal choice and the seminary's corporate acceptance become fused in the seminarian's view of God, his understanding of holiness, and his obedient submission to the will of God personified in the bishop or religious superior. This process is ritualised in the ordination rite when the ordained places his hands between the bishop's hands and promises respect and obedience to his ordinary (bishop or religious superior). By the time the seminarian is ordained, he belongs—at least externally—to the company.

Seminaries do not intentionally ordain mavericks. They appear after ordination when an individual realises the impact of ritualised behaviour and decides how to live with it. When he recognises the institution has no power over him, the ordained has options. He could leave and divest himself of the deep ritualisation, stay and become reconciled to it, or become more ritualised.

Seminary formation teaches priests how to relate and care for others ritually through sacraments and sacramentals, and in other ways too. The ritualised behaviour patterns learned throughout seminary training become, for many, the template for their decision-making and conflict resolution as well. The learned ritual behaviour influences, if not proscribes, a priest's fundamental understanding of the nature and purpose of liturgy, personal prayer, communication, pastoral care, and even recreation. Until a priest learns to worship, pray, communicate, and care in non-ritualised ways, his communication often remains institutional and "sacramentalised" in words and gestures that refer back to the sacraments: "I'll pray for you". Add to the institutional forces those of personality, culture and family, education, spirituality, self-identity (priest and man), and the public role of the priest, and you have the complex persona of "the priest". Depending on who he is "ritually", the man who inhabits the sanctuary will either celebrate the Mass, say the Mass, or preside at the Eucharist.

The proliferation of virtual masses was about the opportunity and the priesthood's value, visibility, and engagement. It was about being seen. For those priests who used forms of online participation in the Sunday Mass, it was also about engagement and inclusion. However, the primary engagement direction was one-way, from the priest to the people, not from the people to the priest. Most clerics did not engage in other forms of online prayer, pastoral discussion or scripture sharing. The majority stayed with the online Mass as their primary experience of "shared prayer".

The virtual Mass became, for many priests, their only effective form of communication, activity, and worship. Their *raison d'etre*. We can identify an operative theology of priesthood that drives liturgy by reflecting on these motivations. What drove the online Mass—and continues to drive it— is not an articulated understanding of liturgical practice or a nuanced theology of the liturgy but a more profound, often unarticulated, almost primal understanding of priesthood.

This picture suggests that contemporary priesthood is exercised both functionally and personally. The Mass is a personal attribute of the priest and a function of his priesthood. In most cases, the personal and the functional are so deeply intertwined in a primal way that one does not have existence without the other. Indeed, 80% of respondents indicated that they used the daily Mass as their primary act of personal prayer. A functionalist approach to priesthood and liturgy is driven by more complex motivations.

I know that many different motivations form an individual priest's approach to Mass, the priesthood, and the sacraments. These are deeply anchored in an individual's image of God, ministry, and self and articulated in the priesthood; priesthood is the "place" where all this comes together in a uniquely human gift of self—given to others—through the Church. It is a worldview that forms a unique standing place: a *tūrangawaewae* or *Sitz im Leben*.[1] Thus, a priest may understand himself as a presbyter-minister, a cultic priest, or a sacerdotal man. Priests are holders of the institution and pastors of souls. For some, this will come with an inner turmoil between keeping the rules and making them flex to fit people's lives.

When it comes to the Mass, some will say the Eucharist belongs to the Church at which they preside. But others will say that the Mass is the offering of the eternal sacrifice. As the sacerdotal intermediary in this cultic transaction, they intercede for the people and the salvation of souls. This transaction must carry on because God must be prayed to and, for some, appeased.

When a priest wrote saying, "I am saying Mass for the intentions of the parish and saving souls…through the Holy Sacrifice of the Mass and the spiritual communion" but wasn't communicating in other "ordinary" ways with his parishioners, I was struck by the functionalism of his approach. His was a quasi-magical understanding of communication and sacramental mediation.

For the cultic priest, saying Mass is a function of his office; for the functionalist cleric, saying Mass is their daily job. For some priests, saying the Mass is their display of orthodoxy. There is security in a functional, ritual approach to Mass in a time of crisis; it is a comforting display of presence and a safe means of communication.

Covid responses have given us a glimpse into the deeper, rarely articulated functionalism that underscores priesthood and how functionalism drives liturgy from the use of words, rituals, and song choices to the inability to change Mass times or manage the closure of churches. Functionalism is a reason why so many priests and bishops—across the globe—continued to celebrate Mass on their own without the presence of the laity. Becoming aware of functionalism, we are challenged to look at the language we use to describe the act of Eucharistic liturgy. Can we distinguish the intentions thus: Does "saying Mass" indicate a functionalist approach to liturgy and "presiding at Eucharist" a non-functionalist approach?

Functionalism is one of the most potent motivators behind the liturgical responses of lockdown. It has contributed to an internalised clericalism in laity and clergy that drives our ecclesial and liturgical life. It appears to be the default setting illustrated in the proliferation of virtual masses. Functionalism is also responsible for the movement away from the stated theology of the Eucharist as the Sunday gathering of the Church to the Mass said alone by the priest or bishop. Functionalism is not the innovation, but its presence indicated the dilemma: can we affirm that when a priest or bishop celebrates Mass alone without a member of the baptised being present, this is the authentic expression of the leitourgia of the Church?

---

1 Tūrangawaewae (noun) domicile, standing, place where one has the right to stand – place where one has rights of residence and belonging through kinship and whakapapa. Sitz im Leben – place where you sit-in-life.

A Disrupted and

Innovated Church

According to Christensen, "'disruptive innovation" doesn't refer to the 'instantaneous value' of a product or service in the market. Instead, it refers to the lifecycle or life over time of the product's behaviour in the market.'[1] Disruption is a process that takes the innovation of the garage to the marketplace and changes the market in the process, like self-publishing. In Christensen's thinking, disruption is creating a new consumer base through accessibility. Disruptive innovation originates in lower-end customer bases, where customers are less demanding. It creates a new market that takes hold because the hegemonic presumptions of the elites are looking elsewhere or are dismissive of the innovation. Thus, new providers—innovators—don't become disruptors until the quality of their product matches the quality of the existing provider.[2] For example, people don't buy at the supermarket deli until they are convinced it is as good or better than their local, established butcher.

Innovation describes how companies enhance the experience, so customers know they are valued. The customer's experiences of being valued and belonging to the "family" of the company is critical. The experiential value of belonging to the "community of customers" keeps them faithful and attracts others. According to Christensen, disruption creates a new "value network". An example of this is the advent of

Netflix rather than Uber. In the world of taxis, Uber is not a disruptor because, while Uber has challenged the taxi business, it has not moved the concept of personal transport in a radically new direction. Uber helped Christensen understand that 'being at the bottom of the market is [not necessarily] the causal mechanism' for innovation or disruption, 'but that it's correlated with a business model that is unattractive to its competitor.'[3] For that, we need to look at Netflix.

The demise of the corner video shop and the cinema's diversification into cafés are examples of Netflix as a disruptive innovation. The Netflix community and the cinema's and the video shop's customer base are related communities of users or customers. The community of movie watchers display the same behaviours—watching movies. Their behaviours are the key to their engagement with each supplier (Netflix, cinema, and video shop) and their use of the supplier's product and service. Before Netflix, the central behaviour was watching movies, either as a cinemagoer or a video shop customer, since Netflix, three common behaviours are movie-watching, choice, and access.

Initially, Netflix did not disrupt the supply of movies to video shops or impact cinemas, nor did it disrupt the behaviour of the movie-going public. Initially, Netflix merely offered another means of sourcing movies through a home postage system. The advantage of Netflix over the cinemas was freedom from movie schedules. Patrons could watch what they liked when they liked. The edge over the video shops was not getting movies back on time to avoid incurring additional fees. Netflix only changed the fundamental behaviour of movie-watchers once it capitalised on internet connectivity. Netflix did not invent the internet or drive people to use it before this. When the behaviour of movie-goers was altered, it impacted both cinemas and video shops. Eventually, the behaviour of watching a movie changed. Once watching a movie was a special occasion, a night out for the family or a date that included physically going to the movie cinema or the video shop. Once the behaviour of movie-watching became possible without physical encounter, the domestic armchair became the venue, and movie-watching became an event that meant never having to leave the house!

As people became familiar and comfortable with their new behaviours of movie watching, they missed some social interaction but wanted to retain the domestic feel of movie-watching. As a result, cinemas changed their configuration. They introduced armchairs, bars and cafes and tried to imitate the home environment. Once alcoholic drinks and coffee were forbidden, now they were promoted as part of the movie-going experience.

To meet the change in movie-watching behaviours, cinemas became "destinations", and the video shops joined the Jurassic age. Movie watching behaviour no longer included the public—except when one visited a cinema. Movie-watching became accessible and international and domestic because one can watch movies from all over the world in every genre, at any time, for a small cost.

We need to consider four concepts from Christensen's work before looking further at Covid lockdown's liturgical and pastoral implications. First, great companies fail because they listen to their customers and seek to provide the mainline customers with more of what they want. Second, businesses introduce sustaining technologies to give the mainline customers more, but sustaining technologies don't move the customer forward. Third, the presence of disruptive technologies; and fourth, the notion of technology as the transfer of 'labor, capital, materials and information into products and services of greater value' to either the mainline customer or the new fringe customer.[4] The link between these is the customer and where they sit on the innovative-disruptive spectrum.

Christensen writes,

> Precisely because these [great] firms listened to their customers, invested aggressively in new technologies that would provide their customers more and better products of the sort they wanted, and because they carefully studied market trends and systematically allocated investment capital to innovations that promised the best returns, they lost their positions of leadership.[5]

Sustaining technologies,

> foster improved product performance. I call these sustaining technologies...What all sustaining technologies have in common is that they improve the performance of established products, along the dimensions of performance that mainstream customers in major markets have historically valued. Most technological advances in a given industry are sustaining in character.6

He describes disruptive technologies as those that,

> bring to a market a very different value proposition than had been available previously. Generally, disruptive technologies underperform established products in mainstream markets. But they have other features that a few fringe (and generally new) customers value.[7]

Liturgical Innovation

The disruption to liturgical and pastoral practice has brought three innovations worth considering.

First, the innovation of the virtual mass with the priest as the sole actor. Second, the innovation of worship without physical proximity and social presence. And third, the innovation of lay home-prayers, including the lay-eucharistic meal.

Each innovation is the result of responding to the dominant customer's wants—Mass—and the dominant provider's needs—priests and pastoral teams—through the introduction of sustaining technologies—virtual masses and online prayers. The transfer of labour, materials, time and talent from the proximate, physical environment to the virtual environment to achieve this has opened the door to disruptive technologies and created the opportunity for disruptive liturgical and pastoral practices to reform our liturgical-sacramental life in significant ways.

The introduction of the Liturgy of the Word with Holy Communion as a sustaining technology to substitute for the Sunday Eucharist has become the disruptive innovation of many parishes and rural communities. What began as an innovation to give priests a day off and the laity an opportunity to lead worship has led to the situation where communities of Catholics will more happily have "their" liturgy on a Sunday rather than travel twenty minutes longer to celebrate the Eucharist. The innovation to sustain small parishes that could not have the Sunday Eucharist because of the scarcity of priests had become the disruptive innovation that threatens established theologies of the local church, the Eucharist, community priesthood and the presumed centrality of the Sunday Eucharist in the life of Catholics.

The innovation of the virtual Mass, like the online prayers, were responses to the dominant customer group's need for prayer and consolation. We spent hours and thousands of dollars sustaining this dominant customer profile—and we continue to do so. We have contributed to a product-focussed, transactional understanding of the liturgy and a functionalist understanding of the priesthood through online and virtual tools. By not calling into question the more significant issue of who the worshipping community is and asking what the impact of all this activity might be on the future, we have created a sustaining technology for the mainstream customers that will ultimately become another problem to solve.

The transference of the "technology of worship" from the physical to the virtual environment has become the means of avoiding not just the risk of physical gathering, but more importantly, the suffering of not being able to gather in a mediated, sacramental way—physically. In doing so, we have created at the fringes non-physical events and home, non-community events that do not need a community beyond the living room.

We have contributed to disrupting our understanding of physical, proximate, mediated, sacramental gathering through using sustaining technologies. The impact of sustaining technologies has turned the Mass into a product that can be distributed to anyone, everywhere in the world, without the requirement to be a participant or even be present, beyond the click of a mouse.

The use of sustaining technology has undoubtedly innovated our delivery of online Masses and other forms of prayer. Still, it has not changed behaviours or the presentation of the ritual form. The sustaining technology of the virtual Mass has relied on the transactional nature of the liturgy and priesthood and the performance elements of ritual. We now have liturgical and products accessible anytime, from anywhere, by anyone. Technology has changed our dominant liturgy and pastoral engagement from physical to digital gatherings.

Part One

Given the enormous impact of sustainable technology, it is easy to conclude that the most significant liturgical change has come through the use of technology, but I'm afraid I have to disagree with this conclusion. The proliferation of virtual and television masses predated Covid. Their large volume during Covid should not distract us because they did not change the foundational liturgical behaviours of priests and laity. On the contrary, they have supported established behaviour. The virtual Mass has promoted a conservative, passive form of worship.

Transferring the Mass from the sanctuary to the internet did not—in the main—include changing its ritual form, structure, vesture, and texts. Virtual mass presentations did not radicalise the viewers or the general Catholic population because they replicated the sanctuary. Virtual masses were not meant to alter liturgical behaviour but to use the performance-based ritual to keep the customers happy and linked in. In this regard, the online or virtual masses were a product that maintained business-as-usual. In this sense, the virtual Mass has been a significant conserving element of worship throughout Covid.

The virtual Mass is not a radicalised form of the Mass. Even at its most innovative, when online audiences said the words of Institution with the priest, the ritual form, texts, and vesture were all retained. The online Mass was a concerted effort to carry on business as usual and to provide the parishioners with a tried, trustworthy, reliable, and recognisable form of worship. It was served up the same on every continent. We have not out-McDonalded McDonalds; we got there first. The Catholic Church created the model of the pre-packaged, internationally delivered, supra-cultural form of meeting and eating! The impact of this approach has been to signal that the Mass is a standard package delivered via the internet and accessible anywhere in the world from anywhere across the globe.

Virtual worship has shown the laity virtually and physically excluded from worship and the dominance of the priest-presider. Including spiritual communion for the laity, while the priest ate and drank alone, is a pattern of exclusion or hegemony. Sadly, the desire to give consolation to the laity has not worked because it is paternalistic. The paternalism continues with the initiatives of walk-up communion and takeaway communion. If there is an innovation here, it is the innovation of choice.

If anything, the virtual Mass has unwittingly contributed to the liturgical disruption of the physical liturgical community through taking the viewer from the pew to the couch and showing that liturgy in its present form and experience is not essentially a communitarian experience and through offering unlimited choice. The Netflix reformation equivalent was not taking the Mass online but facilitating its move away from its physical environment—from the cinema to the armchair and from the local video shop to the living room. The online or virtual masses have removed the physicality of engagement and reduced the user to a passive observer. It has done this because it has not challenged, changed, or radicalised liturgical behaviours. Indeed, the online Mass has traded on established, transactional behaviours.

The virtual Mass has not innovated worship in any way; if anything, it has put it back hundreds of years. Virtual masses have hooked into a pre-existing form of liturgical behaviour that does not require the presence of the People of God in their hierarchical character. In doing so, virtual masses have exposed the operative theology of liturgy that actually underpins the majority of catholic liturgical practice. Consequently, the proliferation of virtual masses is not the critical disruptor; it is more Uber than Netflix.

Liturgical Disruption

The driver of liturgical innovation resulting from Covid-19 has been the disruption to the physical, human gathering. The disruption to physical, social communities is based on the fundamental assumption that physical gatherings inside buildings pose a danger to personal health and public safety. The disruption to physical, communitarian activities impacted the liturgical experience. Liturgy requires physical presence and uses rituals that bind priests, people, music, communion, touch, song, prayer, eating and drinking in a profound, physically expressed communion. The disruption to physical gatherings has brought innovation. We have also innovated participation through our need to accommodate our loss of physical community. At the same time, we have lost liturgy's foundational conscious and active involvement.

Physical gathering and social identity go hand-in-hand. Physical gatherings rely on physical safety, and this is no longer assured. Church congregations are considered to be potential super-spreaders of infection. Thus, for me, the critical disruptor of parish life is not the virtual Mass nor the online prayer opportunities but the prohibition against physical and social gatherings. This prohibition continues to frame individuals' considerations of returning to Mass. People are now more wary of community gatherings and physical touch. Sacramental practises and liturgical gestures that require physical contact, such as sharing the chalice shaking hands at the Sign of Peace, may be gone forever.

The prohibitions against physical gatherings have also fired our innovation and brought several new liturgical resources, but the most significant loss is the mediated sacramental experience.

Our sacramental mediation requires touch, intimacy, proximity, and physicality. Physical distancing, the wearing of masks, communion from behind a screen, prohibitions on singing, limited numbers at masses, and virtual masses have all contributed to changing our appreciation for physical community and our liturgical participation.

When we stand, chatting, after Mass in the car park without a mask and close to each other—having just attended Mass wearing a mask and being physically distanced from others—we realise that worship, church and community are dangerous, and it's safer not to participate. By contrast, our behaviour outside says, "this is safe".

Where the human community is a threat to our well-being, we also realise the need to innovate the community so that it is not a source of danger or risk. Thus, while believers can find a safe liturgical community online, they cannot do it in their local church. The disruption to the foundational presumptions of communitarian worship is the most important innovation of the liturgy during the Covid liturgical reform.

The most significant disruptive innovation that may escape attention is lay-led worship. The home became the place of worship either when people watched a Mass or performed their own Sunday liturgy. In schools, the classroom teachers and the senior students became the new, available, and safe worship leaders. This was necessary because the sacramental system's mediation through a priest was unavailable.

Lay-led worship has allowed many to radically rework worship through democratised liturgical forms with a flat leadership model and an inclusive prayer form. These prayer forms allow people to use non-standard liturgical texts, where participants and leaders do not feel obliged to maintain or use standard liturgical patterns and ritual texts. For example, it is possible to substitute the Our Father for a text addressed to "Our Heavenly Parent" or "Mother and Father God".

The disruptive innovation has transferred the necessity of the ordained mediator to a new group of mediators through the virtue of necessity. And, because these lay-led "Covid forms" are democratised and not priest-centric, they are not exclusively sacrament. As lay-led "covid liturgical forms", they facilitate lay presiding and question the exclusive rights of ordained presiders. These forms are also more localised or congregational in form and substance because they are not attempting to traverse the entire Catholic world. This is the disruptive liturgical innovation of Covid.

This form of worship leadership will become stronger in the long term because it will be seen as the more viable option for those on the fringe and for mainstream parishioners.

In 2020, and more strongly in 2021, we noticed a marked fall-off in mass attendance and pastoral life participation. Partly, this is due to the loss of habitual practices. The return to business as usual, which was stronger in 2020, was less evident in 2021. After the second extended lockdown of 2021 (August 17 to September 7), our churches remained closed for public masses for another two weeks because of the transmissibility of the delta variant. Since then, the take up of home-based liturgies has increased, and mass attendance has dramatically decreased. Parishioners have become "more content" with worship away from the Church.

When we consider this experience using Christensen's framework, we see that we have used sustaining technologies to keep ourselves in business during the pandemic. Consequently, too few priests stepped back and asked the question: is all prayer liturgy, or is there a reality to the

Sacred Liturgy that takes it beyond mere ritualisation? We turned the Mass into a form of Covid-communication and reached back to pre-Vatican thinking to achieve this. I think this happened because the transactional, performative drivers of worship and priesthood took over.

Online masses display the operative, transactional theology; it is not just a response to Covid. The transactional mindset (shared by laity and clergy) sees the priest as the cultic surrogate and the people as the recipients of quasi-magical graces and effects.

The institutionalised model is widespread and deeply engrained. This model's operative theology drove much of the "liturgical innovation". It was easier to turn the liturgy into a product than imagine other alternatives.

---

[1] Clayton M. Christensen; Michael E. Raynor; Rory McDonald, "What Is Disruptive Innovation?" Harvard Business Review, retrieved 25 October 2021.

2 Forrest, Conner, https://www.techrepublic.com/article/startup-jargon-10-terms-to-stop-using/, retrieved 2 May 2021.

3 Susan, Adams, "Clayton Christensen On What He Got Wrong About Disruptive Innovation". Forbes, retrieved 12 October 2021.

4 Christensen, The Innovator's Dilemma, xvii.

5 Christensen, xvi.

6 Christensen, xix.

7 Christensen, xix.

PART TWO

LITURGICAL

THEOLOGY

Sacrosanctum Concilium

The Second Vatican Council's Constitution on the Sacred Liturgy, *Sacrosanctum Concilium* (1963), guides my theology of liturgy.[1] It underpins the following exploration of the problems I see with many of the prayer innovations used throughout liturgical lockdown. *Sacrosanctum Concilium* is the basis of the sacramental theology I used here. From this source emerges my theology of the liturgy and my theology of liturgical praxis. *Sacrosanctum Concilium* is a lens through which I understand the theological concept of leitourgia or service of God in worship. Leitourgia is the term that best expresses my understanding of sacramental worship and mediation. Leitourgia is the act that articulates thanks to God for the salvation given by God to humankind. It grounds the central principle of *participatio actuosa* or active participation and establishes the necessity for liturgical presence.

In this part, my attention is focussed on the negative impact of most Covid liturgical responses that have neglected the central principle of *participatio actuosa* of the 1970 Roman Missal of Pope Paul VI, or the Pauline Liturgy and consequently ignored the notion of liturgical presence. Televising the 1962 Roman Missal is not my concern here. Unlike the 1970 Missal, the 1962 Missal has no theological requirement or expectation for the inclusion and participation of the assembly using the principle of *participatio actuosa*. In fact, it is the perfect form for televised and virtual masses and the authentic context for non-participative "spiritual communion". However, the theological requirement for active participation and shared participation—by the laity and the priest—in the celebration of the Mass is central to the 1970 Missal. Because the ritual presumptions of the unreformed rite have made their way into the practice of the reformed rite, the communion ecclesiology of the 1970 Roman Missal has been undermined.

The reasons lie in the post-conciliar use of the 1962 and 1970 Roman Missals. Between 2007 and 2021, the Mass was couched as having an Ordinary (Pauline) and an Extraordinary (Latin) Form created by Pope Benedict XVI.[2] This distinction was rescinded by Pope Francis in 2021 when the Church returned to one form of the lex orandi, the Mass of Pope St. Paul VI.

Before Covid, televised masses were used in some countries, like the United States, Great Britain, and France, to drive the agenda of progressives, centrist, right-of-centre and extreme right-wing groups. While televised masses were also used for pastoral reasons, such as for the sick in hospitals, this did not stop groups from weaponising the Mass as part of their Catholic culture war.

Several terms that I frequently use may be unfamiliar to some readers. These are leitourgia, mysterion, anamnesis and lex orandi, lex credendi. Translated, they are liturgy, mystery, remembrance and the law of prayer and belief. Each is critical to our understanding of liturgy, and the celebration of sacraments, especially the Mass or the Sacred Liturgy.

These words are more than just specialist terms. They articulate the theological experience that underpins our sacramental system. They help us understand the experience of sacramental meditation and the broader concept of sacramentality.

I use leitourgia, mysterion, lex orandi, lex credendi, and anamnesis because I want to take you—the reader—into a deeper reflection on the nature of the liturgy. These words open up liturgy's history, purpose, and human and divine dimensions. They enable us to explore the nature and practice of liturgy theologically and anthropologically. These specialist words unlock the word "liturgy" and rescue it from meaning too many different things to too many people.

Leitourgia, mysterion, anamnesis and lex orandi, lex credendi, take us deeper into our understanding of, and belief in, the Incarnation and the Trinity. In the context of this book, they are critical for a fuller discussion of (1) the problem posed by virtual Mass, (2) the theology of the laity in the liturgy, and (3) the operative, transactional theology of the Eucharist, which we use.

Leitourgia is a Greek term meaning "work by the people for the larger population". It is a composite term from Greek civic life for people (*laos*) and task (*ergon*). It refers to anyone who performs a public duty. In its original context, leitourgia (λειτουργία) can mean a public office undertaken by a citizen at their own expense or a service (military, workmen) for the good of the city. Its biblical usage includes the service or ministry of cultic or temple priests. It can include the sacrifices offered to God or a gift or benefaction for the relief of the needy.[3]

Leitourgia applied to the intention of Christian worship states that we—believers—pray for all people and on behalf of all people. It also has a deeper meaning when applied to God; it is the service of God for the created order. The German word *Gottesdienst* or "God's service" is applicable here. It offers us the opportunity to consider leitourgia as a divine-to-human service and a human-to-divine service simultaneously without excluding one or the other. Who serves whom? God serves us, and we serve God.

Mysterion is a Greek term meaning "the hidden thing" confided only to the believer. Mysterion is the hidden purpose or counsel of something greater that gives meaning to something else, such as human life, or it articulates the presence of the divine. The English word mystery is problematic because it suggests a problem to be solved rather than a wonder to be encountered. Mysterion emphasises that leitourgia is a work that explores and articulates the mysterion. Through it, believers come to know the presence of the divine.

Anamnesis is a Greek term meaning active remembering and is the opposite of amnesia. Anamnesis is "dynamic memory". The "memory" of Christ as he stands before the Father is the "dynamic memory" of salvation, and this "memory" is the memory of the Church, who is the keeper of the memory. The work of leitourgia articulates the anamnesis of the Church that proclaims the mysterion of salvation.

Lex orandi and lex credendi are two Latin terms that work as a single unit. Prayer (orandi) proposes, or presents, belief (credendi) because our prayer is a catechetical experience. Prayer and belief form a unity of praying and believing because one can only pray what one believes and believe what one prays. For example, we learn to sign ourselves as children with the Sign of Cross for our prayers at home and church. In this action, we learn the rule of prayer as we learn the rule of belief: God is Trinity; God is Father, Son and Spirit; prayer is bodily and verbal; prayer is private and personal; prayer is public and corporate.

When we pray liturgically, we express our belief through rituals, symbols, and signs, of which the Sign of the Cross is an example. It is a liturgical action that represents the mysterion of salvation brought to anamnesis (mind) in the physical act of making the Sign of the Cross.

The Sign of the Cross is both a prayer and a sign of belief. Only a believer can make the Sign of the Cross and believe in it, confirming the relationship between—what is prayed and what is believed—the lex orandi and the lex credendi. This single action articulates in ritual form belief in the Incarnation, the Crucifixion, and the Trinity that is both personal and corporate. I cannot make the Sign of the Cross without belonging to the community of faith because "my faith" is "their faith", even when I bless myself at home in private, it is an act of the community's or the Christian Church's faith.

Liturgy – An Image of Immersion

The liturgy is a complex reality. Liturgy is like a swimming pool with a shallow end and a deep end. At the shallow end, it appears easy to understand. It is a list of ritual actions, postures, and gestures. It is a choice of style or mode. There are words to say, clothes to wear and songs to sing. All these elements are held together through the performance itself. At this level, liturgy is something we "do". It is primarily a list of tasks performed by different actors in a ritual sequence.

Towards the middle of the pool—where the head is still just above the water—all the ritual actions, vestments, words, postures, gestures, and songs take on a deeper meaning. However, one senses that the performance is losing its overriding power, and style is less important. One is more aware of a spiritual need to *be* prayer, not just *attend at* prayer. In this place, one sees the ritual actions, vestments, words, postures, gestures, and songs through their individual histories and interrelationships. They are instructive elements of the presence of God, but none of them "are God".

Once one becomes more aware of the presence of God through the absence of ritual elements, one experiences the call to leave behind *liturgy-as-my-service-for God* and enter *liturgy-as-service-by-God* to the world. This awareness changes what has been a call to performance into a call to vocation and participation in the liturgy as God's service. With one's head just above the water, one is aware of a deeper relationship that makes liturgy sacramental and the whole of creation the object of God's Grace. One is beginning to enter a relationship of leitourgia. Liturgical participation changes from function to transformation.

At the deepest end of the pool, the styles of the ritual actions with their vesture, postures, gestures, songs, and words are less critical to the point of being unnecessary. Whereas at the shallow end, a person will see the unlit candles on the altar and rush up during the Gospel to light them, at the deeper end, one doesn't see or even need candles. The predominant symbol is one's own immersion into the depths of the life of God, being in over one's head. Here God is the one who serves, and we, as believers, participate in that original leitourgia through our anamnesis of the Trinity's "work" in the Paschal Mystery. We are served or ministered to by God, and we respond from a place of humility and acceptance.

As the water covers the head, human air, breathing, oxygen, and meaning are unimportant. In this experience, one begins to learn to breathe underwater. It is a mystical experience; the place of the mysterion is a place of inclusion in the life of God. The air one breathes is the Paschal Mystery itself; not an understanding of it, or preferred style of vesture, postures, gestures, songs, and words that express it, but the *Mysterion* itself! What is argued over at the shallow end doesn't make it to the deeper end.

The journey to the deepest end of the pool begins in the shallow end. At this end, one learns how to participate guided by ritual using vesture, postures, gestures, songs, and words. This is the structure that we need to learn. Until we worship in "spirit and in truth" in the presence of God, we need symbols. But not everyone needs the same amount of symbolisation; for example, some need songs, incense, and vesture while some need only the presence of others. Symbols are needed—but not ultimately—as participatory rituals and shared forms that express our unity as a body of believers. As participative symbols, they are not intended for singular use by an individual; they are the symbols of a pilgrim people. They articulate things about God, but they are not God. Using them, we stand with Christ, before the Father, in the power of the Holy Spirit. They are participative symbols and alert us to their ultimate meaning and purpose. They gather people before God and enable doxology!

Once one has experienced the deepest end of the liturgy, one will yearn for it again and often not find it; this is the "dark night of leitourgia". Comprehension of leitourgia from its shallowest (performance liturgy) to its deepest end (leitourgia) requires participation in the cultic forms without reducing liturgy or leitourgia to a "mere" cult. Although liturgy/leitourgia is a ritual function, it is not a "sacred communication" cult that transacts with the deity in a commercial sense to exchange goods and services for payment and loyalty. Instead, liturgy/leitourgia celebrates a more significant, existing reality using anamnesis (living, continual memory) in a cultic form.

The notion of Christian leitourgia creates a cultic antinomy between the radical abolition of religious cults, their cultic priesthoods and sacrificial transaction while using cultic expressions to express our belief in our God, who is the final sacrifice who establishes eschatological life and ends the need for cultic priesthoods, temples and sacrifices; 'The Christian leitourgia is not a "cult" if by this term we mean a sacred action, or rite, performed in order to establish "contact" between the community and God'.[4]

Christian liturgy is our response to the mysterion of God's work of salvation. It orientates us to God as the source of the mysterion and the summit of its expression in Christ. Liturgy is not a cultic act that re-transacts salvation each time it is celebrated as if the eternal fight between good and evil was still up for grabs. The Eucharist isn't celebrated every Sunday to update or restate the promise of salvation as if God has forgotten. Every Sunday, the Eucharist is celebrated to remind believers of their blessing and keep them in touch with the mysterion they believe in. Our praise adds nothing to God's greatness but helps us grow in holiness.[5]

Unlike the cultic elements in the contemporary sacrificial culture of the media or the historical temple cults with their high priests of sacrifice and their rituals of sin atonement, the Christian liturgy's only priest and only sacrifice is Christ himself. Christian worship is "done" in Christ, through Christ, and with Christ, and believers participate in the eternal event of the Paschal Mystery through anamnesis. Robert Taft has written about St Paul that he never used the 'cultic nomenclature (liturgy, sacrifice, priest, offering) for anything but a life of self-giving, lived after the pattern of Christ. When he does speak of what we call liturgy...he makes it clear that its purpose is to contribute to this "liturgy of life"'.[6]

As Romano Guardini has written, 'The way to liturgical living does not just go via instruction, but rather before all through the action.'[7] Liturgy is a theological and anthropological activity. It is the activity within which communication occurs using its own vocabulary of words, signs, and symbols that communicate the inner truth of the belief being celebrated. But long before liturgy becomes a ritualised, shared experience, it is first a primary or primal experience. We are already praying before we understand rituals, rites, and liturgical forms. The primal form of worship becomes theologised the more we think about it.

When one begins to think about the purpose of liturgy and the Church as a phenomenon, one looks for a Theology *of the* Liturgy and ultimately a theology of God. When one begins by asking, "what am I doing here at Mass?" or "why am I not at church?". One seeks to understand the purpose of liturgy and the one one is praying to. This is the beginning of a dialogue between an individual and God. It may occur within the community or to its side. Generally, people approach these questions through the experience of shared worship or through its absence. Either way, the community of worshippers plays a part and cannot be avoided. Thus, for most people, their search for a Theology *of the* Liturgy goes via their experience of liturgical prayer.

The search for a theology of liturgy is generally the search for a community to believe in. It is the search for an ecclesiology or a theology of the Church or the Body Catholic because participation in Christian liturgy is foundationally ecclesiological. This is why Pope Francis, in his recent *Moto Proprio, Traditionis Custodes*, is absolutely correct to restate there is only one unique form of the lex orandi in the Latin Rite: The Roman Missal of 1970.

Liturgical prayer in its public form requires shared liturgical participation in its ecclesiological symbols. Where this is not present, divisions cannot be avoided, and unity is not expressed. At this point, an individual wants to know who they are worshipping and whether the God proposed to them for belief by the community—the Catholic Church—is believable? Who am I worshipping with, and who is the one we are worshipping? When one begins to ask these questions, one seeks a Theology of Liturgical Praxis.

Theologies of liturgical praxis and theologies of the liturgy are essential if an individual and a community of believers are to be authentic expressions of the faith of the Church in human life. Because the liturgy is an action of human beings, theologies of the liturgy and liturgical praxis must include robust liturgical anthropologies. Because liturgy is the participative action of consecrated people in the life and work of God, its anthropology must be Christian and rooted in scripture. Theology and Christian anthropology enable us to worship authentically and to comprehend culture and cult. They guide us to understand the dynamic of liturgy as part of the more significant experience of salvation because *believers* participate in the liturgy as *human beings*.

We are recipients of God's work of salvation—the sanctification of all things and the inclusion of all things into the life of God—and we are the messengers of this Good News. The human and the divine form a single "work" in worship. The "work" of God is the "service" God gives to the world, a service of salvation and redemption. Christians are called into the leitourgia of God through baptism. God is the initiator, and we are the recipients of this leitourgia. We respond to God's leitourgia through our liturgy of worship. Liturgy has an ontological basis—or being—that ultimately finds its origin in God; thus, liturgy acts as a source of theology. We can use the liturgy—nature, purpose, source—to understand why God's leitourgia (liturgy or service) is "an event" that happens in time and space.

Because the Church's liturgy—as locus and experience of salvation—is linked to God's leitourgia, it is a place or source of Grace and salvation through an encounter with Christ in the Church. Our liturgy is an event in time and space that responds to this initial work of God, and it is the frame through which we know the meaning of the Church's leitourgia of sacraments, evangelisation, and sanctification. The more we know liturgy as participation in the leitourgia of God, the more we can live lives within God's leitourgia of salvation.

---

[1] SC., 2, p.117.

2 Ordinary and Extraordinary forms was a term coined by Pope Benedict XVI in Summorum Pontificum (2007) and abrogated by Pope Francis in Traditiones Custodes (2021). It is used here because it was still an operative terminology at the time of Covid-19 in 2020.

3 Its elements are leitos (from leos = laos, or people) meaning public, and ergo (obsolete in the present stem, used in future erxo, etc.) meaning to do. From this we have leitourgos, "a

man who performs a public duty", "a public servant", often used as equivalent to the Roman lictor; then leitourgeo, "to do such a duty", leitourgema, its performance, and leitourgia, the public duty itself. Catholic Encyclopaedia http://www.newadvent.org/cathen/09306a.htm (accessed 4 January 2010).

4 Alexander Schmemann, "Liturgical Theology, Theology of Liturgy and Liturgical Reform," in Liturgy and Tradition: Theological Reflections of Alexander Schmemann, ed. Thomas Fisch (Crestwood, New York: St Vladimir's Seminary Press, 1990), 40.

5 Common Preface IV, in The Roman Missal, English Translation, Third Typical Edition, Wellington, 2010, 621.

6 Robert Taft, "Towards a Theology of the Christian Feast," Beyond East & West, Problems in Liturgical Understanding (Washington, DC: The Pastoral Press, 1984) 5, in David Fagerberg, Theologica Prima. What Is Liturgical Theology? (2nd ed.), Hillenbrand Books, Chicago/Mundelein, Illinois, 2004, 13.

7 Romano Guardini, Von heiligen Zeichen, 8.9, 'Der Weg zu liturgischem Leben geht eben nicht durch bloße Belehrung, sondern er geht vor allem durch das Tun.' My translation.

Theology of Praxis

When talking about sacred liturgy, everything begins and ends in God. When we speak like this, we are talking theology. Sacred liturgy cannot be "done" without "doing" theology, and this is a trap that people sometimes fall into; they try to "do" liturgy as a human activity. When we talk of liturgy as a human activity—which is not wrong—it is work done by some of the population on behalf of all the people.

The celebration of Christian liturgy celebrates all of human life for the Christian person and the Christian community. Liturgy is a complex interplay of experience, ritual, intellect, prayer, and performance. It is an expressive act that brings a believer's faith to the surface. In Christian liturgy, we pray what we believe, and in our prayer, our belief takes on ritual and expressive form. Liturgy is an interplay of personal and corporate expressions of worship and faith. It is the place where we pray with others.

Liturgy is the place of theology, or more specifically, the ground of theology, where you stand and from where you give praise to God. Liturgy requires theology. It gives birth to theology, and it is theology enacted. Because theology is not like a pre-cooked dinner bought from the supermarket or a pizza delivered, it needs time. Just as liturgy gives ritual language to belief, theology at various levels provides the language and concepts we need to express what liturgy means and does. For each person to develop theologically, they must (1) develop a personal theology of seeking God and of desiring to be known by God; (2) experience their shared primal humanness that seeks meaning and expression through ritualisation; (3) experience their individual "I" as insufficient to the task of finding meaning; and (4), if they are to find a place in the communal expression of liturgy to learn how to locate their "I" within the "us" of the community to live out of the revelation of the "WE" of God.

I hope the following analogy from the world of sport illustrates the problem we face when we use online worship forms without considering the unintended consequences of the action.

A Game of Sport

Consider an international game of rugby between the All Blacks and the Springboks.[1] The liturgy begins at home for the fan and in the hotel room for the player, but we will concentrate on the fan. The fan dresses in their fan clothing, with the scarf, hat, flag, and begins the procession to the stadium. They join other fans on the way to the stadium. The individual "I" becomes part of the collect "we"; they are no longer individuals; they are now individuals-in-communion. They are fans!

As fans, they belong to each other and the game; and the game belongs to them. They are invested in the outcome and begin to transfer their individual and corporate identity to the game and the team that will play it on their behalf. No longer an individual, their individual "I's" have become the "us" of the group. In this new identity, they will suffer the pain of defeat or the blessings of victory. Our fan joins others, and they enter the stadium, taking their seats among the devoted. No one will leave this event today unchanged.

The pre-liturgy entertainment is loud, all-embracing, and declarative of the life-changing event that is about to take place. The congregation is forming as it sits and waits. The opening rite begins, and the community stands to welcome the chosen who will play on their behalf as their ministers, priests, and bishops. The opening ceremonies declare the difference between the two priestly teams and who they represent and for whom they give their bodies in the liturgy.

The congregation, on its feet, honours the teams as they enter. The teams take their places in the middle of the field, and the national hymns begin. These songs define the purpose of the gathering. They define the fans and give solemnity to an international event. The anthems strengthen the national character, taking the fan from observer to patriot and more profound identification with their teams.

The national anthems are statements of peculiarity that give the players and their fans words to express their solidarity and uniqueness. The hymns are essentially and exclusionary because the anthems belong to one side or the other, not both. They are oppositional hymns that give a sacred sense of purpose through ritual exclusion—only the devotee or believer can sing their song. For Aotearoa, New Zealand, the enculturated rite of the Haka begins. It is a challenge to warfare and a warning that is—hopefully—made good.

Now the congregation has been brought to order, the work of the liturgy can begin. The liturgy is now over to the clergy on the field. They are the ones who must make good the promise of sacred success or face the wrath of the fans through a holy rite of scapegoating— "he's not fit for the game" or "the referee is useless!" The bishop blows the whistle, and the priests begin their rite of conflictual worship, assisted by the ministers at the sideline.

Commentators honour the prowess of individual priests or critique their lack of orthodoxy when they fail to worship according to their expectations of orthodoxy and orthopraxis. The priests fight the good battle on behalf of their supporters, and the bishops control the struggle. The ritualised combat prevents everyone from going to war individually with each other. The violence of the field is accepted, rejoiced in, and permitted. For the crowd, it is violence by proxy. Young, virile men take up the yoke for older, weaker men who remember their days as warriors. These young men are idolised by young, virile women and treated as surrogate sons-of-victory by older women. Everyone is invested in the game because it is much more than just a game.

The congregation, meanwhile, is fully engaged as participants until they realise that nothing they can say or yell from the stands will change the flow and or outcome of the game. There is nothing they can "do" to influence the game. The priests are in charge of the result, and the bishop is directing them while they, the congregation, watch and wait. The assembly is fully conscious, active, and participating, but not in the game itself but in their version of the game, the one they see from the stand. The fans participate vicariously through their emotional connection to the game, the players, the referee, or the opposing team. The fans begin to understand they are not playing the teams' game on the field when they realise that the game is between the priests and they are onlookers. In religious terms, the fan is part of a congregation attending the priest's Mass and observing Father as he prays his Mass; they are not praying with him. The teams play for the fans on the field but not *with* the fans.

In this scenario of public leitourgia, the assembly is one with the priests in spirit but not in action. On the field, the priests are aware of the congregation and want to do everything "for them"—so that they don't go home empty-handed—but they are not "with them". The priests do this service for the people. The players and referees on the field are a singular entity and unity.

The bishop calls an end to the game, and one side is victorious and the other defeated. One drinks from the cup of blessing, and the other does not get a drop! The post-communion prayer is given by the captains, and the embolism (Lt. *Embolismus*) by the commentators. The congregation has already begun to disperse, some to happiness and a communal celebration and others to misery and soul-searching. Because no one leaves this liturgy unchanged, neither does a fan. Their corporate identity fades as they re-enter the world of multiple relationships. The journey home includes shedding the corporate identity of the fan and becoming the lone believer again.

For others, the game was only ever an individual transaction between themselves and the priests on the field. These people never intended to commit themselves to the assembly or the priests. The priests and the congregation serve another narcissistic purpose. Such people are not participants. They shun the reality of corporate identity and create a personalised identity that they control. They do not want to be included in the assembly of the fans at any level beyond the transactional level of being a member of the fan base and permitted to use the word "fan" to get a seat in the stadium. They are fans in name only, present only for themselves. They use the experience vicariously and in a predatory fashion as voyeurs.

For the teams on the field, the fans are nice to have but not essential. As we have seen throughout 2020 and at the 2020 Olympic Games held in 2021 in Tokyo, Japan, fans are unnecessary for sport. The games went on because the action of sport and its competition does not occur between the fans and the sportspeople, but between the sportspeople themselves—the absolute non-necessity of fans is explicit. Fans are not essential to the game or competition. The Olympics without spectators shows that all sport, in the end, is only about the sportsman or woman. While some competitors might feel that they have "lost" something by not having fans present, this is only true at an emotional level. It is not true at a fundamental level of reality or actuality; at the level of ontology!

In the final analysis, the success or failure of the sportsperson or sports team has nothing to do with the presence or absence of the fans. The fans are irrelevant to the outcome unless they get out of the stands and run on the track. Then they are either a competitor or a nuisance!

Because sport can be played without the physical presence of fans, fans have become virtual spectators. They have continued to participate in almost precisely the same way as if they had been physically present in the stands; they have looked on. Instead of participating as "lookers-on" from their stadium seats, they are now lookers-on via their television sets, at another level of abstraction and physical distance. In the end, the fans don't even provide the atmosphere for the sportsperson. The fan's virtual presence confirms that the civic leitourgia of the teams is not primarily or organically related to the crowd. Instead, it is an exclusive action for others that does not require their physical presence. Many would say the Olympics needs a sacred place and a sacred space to be truly itself. The Sacred Liturgy, too, needs its sacred place and its sacred space to express its inner, divine truth.

Sacred Liturgy

The difference between sacred leitourgia and civic leitourgia is Christian leitourgia's christological dimension of *diakonia*—self-giving service—and *martyria*—self-giving sacrifice. The origin of Christian service is revealed in the doctrines of the Trinity and the Incarnation:

> The invisible God, from the fullness of his love, addresses men and women as his friends, and lives among them, in order to invite and receive them into his own company. The pattern of this revelation unfolds through deeds and words which are intrinsically connected: the works performed by God in the history of salvation show forth and confirm the doctrine and realities signified by the words; the words for their part, proclaim the works and bring to the light the mystery they contain.[2]

Christianity's use of leitourgia relies on this revelation. The early Church's application of leitourgia acknowledges God's self-revelation in the divine-human drama of Jesus of Nazareth's life, his death on the cross and the resurrection of the Christ of God. Which we call the Paschal Mystery. The resurrected Christ is the icon of divine leitourgia. Christ announces that all things are made new, fulfilling all promises. He is the 'speaking forth' of the Trinity; thus, everything we do, say, believe, and proclaim in Christian worship is trinitarian. Christian liturgy declares that the Church is the manifestation of the new age, the Kingdom of God. Liturgy is the Paschal Mystery articulated sacramentally in time and space: 'liturgy is not the religion of Christians; liturgy is the religion of Christ perpetuated in Christians'.[3]

The work of salvation or leitourgia begins and ends in God, Father, Son and Holy Spirit. Salvation comes to us from the triune God; we worship the Trinity. Salvation is always the "work" of the Trinity. The Trinity is the source of all sacraments because God is the source and creator of the relationship that creates and sustains them. Thus, sacraments are more than ritual actions or liturgical rites. They are more than "things" to be received or "things" to be given. They are the relational expressions of the presence of God in the world through the Church. Because sacraments and sacramentality are relational, they need to be expressed exteriorly in rites that require physicality in space, movement, gesture, posture.

From within this "original" leitourgia, we who are baptised into Christ participate in the life of God within the *communio* of the Church. In this *communio*, we "remember" God's work of salvation of all creation. We see that God is leitourgia because God is the source of Christian service. God is the one to whom we Christians look and the one to whom we respond with worship.

The Church's leitourgia or service of sacraments, worship and evangelisation is revealed in the divine-human person, Jesus of Nazareth, the Christ of God. His leitourgia, *martyria*, and *diakonia* are both human and divine. At this point, we enter the mysterion of the Paschal Mystery. This overarching phrase expresses the pre-existence, birth, life, death, resurrection, ascension, and second coming of Christ. The

Paschal Mystery speaks to us of the will and work of God.

The community of the baptised, or the Church, is the community of people called to participate in God's work of redemption *in Christ.* The worship of the Church is humankind's response to the presence and action of God in the world, saving us in Christ. Our collective response, or the "us" of the Church, is a single voice made of many individual voices. It is the voice of those who have given their individualist "I" away and joined the "us" of worship.

St Paul's writings articulate the belief that everything living responds to God in Christ because everything exists in and of Christ, in God. The "us" who responds to God is larger than the number of people who go to church because the "us" who responds is all creation. All creation awaits its freedom in Christ: 'Therefore, if anyone is in Christ, he is a new creation; the old has gone, the new has come!'(2 Corinthians 5:17).

Our worship "actively remembers" God's ongoing salvation of the world and actively engages with the Paschal Mystery at many levels. In the liturgy, the Church remembers—with the mind of Christ—all that Jesus did and what Jesus' life, ministry, death, resurrection, and second coming means *to* God. The sacramental rites enable us to participate in Christ's memory of God's leitourgia as he has lived it. It is the "memory" that is continuously revealed throughout human history and is continually saving. Active memory or anamnesis drives the liturgical rites, making them utterly pastoral because they are utterly of Christ.

What distinguishes Sunday liturgy from the liturgy of the stadium is that Sunday liturgy has no spectators or fans; it has only players. Though distinct in their roles and ministries, the clergy and the laity are one, active body. Sadly, when Sunday worship mirrors the stadium, the laity is reduced to an audience. The priests become the only actors on the field. Where this happens, everyone has stepped back from the conciliar theology of worship to a pre-conciliar understanding that places the priest as the surrogate of the faithful, with the result that the liturgy is not 'seen as an exercise of the priestly office of Jesus Christ' but of the priestly elite.[4]

---

1 The All Blacks are the national rugby football team of Aotearoa New Zealand, the Springboks the national team of the Republic of South Africa.
2 Dogmatic Constitution on Divine Revelation, Dei Verbum, 18 November 1965, in 1965 in The Basic Sixteen Documents, Vatican II, Constitutions, Decrees, Declarations, A. Flannery, ed., (New York, Dublin: Costello Publishing and Dominican Publications,1996), 98.
3 Fagerburg, 14.
4 SC., 7, 121.

Priesthood's Operative Theology

Our Covid liturgical responses have unmasked our operative theology of liturgy, priesthood and eucharistic participation. They have exposed the primary motivations for the move to virtual masses and clarified why it was easy. Although the virtual Mass has given us the new flexibility to sit and participate without leaving home, is its flexibility illustrative of a passivity operative in our liturgical praxis?

In this section, I sketch some reasons we saw a proliferation in virtual masses and consider the impact of priests on this trend. . The distinction between virtual and liturgical worship requires understanding the nature of proximate, communal liturgical presence and the non-proximate communication of virtual realities. To make this distinction clearer, I have chosen to use the term virtual Mass instead of online Mass because online systems are functions of cyber communications and virtual environments are considered more than just online or cyber communication. Virtual communications indicate the presence of one person to another who is online.

Another critical element in the operative theology of priesthood is the ritual or cultic transaction culture. If the Mass and the sacraments are understood transactionally, they tend to be reduced to magic articulated through ritual functionaries and formulas. Where this happened, an individualistic approach to worship is often dominant. A transactional approach to liturgy separates its ontological and experiential aspects. Sacraments become either an "experience" or a predominantly "spiritualised" event, having lost their grounding, ecclesial dimension. The separation of the ontological and experiential dimensions refashions liturgy as a product of Christian living. Separating the experiential and ontological dimensions created the drive-in communion. It is responsible in part for the proliferation of the virtual Mass.

The Decree in Time of Covid-19

In March 2020, the Vatican's Congregation for Divine Worship and the Discipline of the Sacraments published its "Decree in Time of Covid-19". It raised significant concerns regarding the theology of the baptised as participants in the liturgical life of the Church, most notably in the celebration of the Eucharist and at the Paschal Triduum. It is an excellent example of liturgical transactional thinking and the operative theology that drove most Covid-19 liturgical responses.

The Decree's central concern is to affirm that priests and bishops can say Mass alone, even at the Easter Triduum. It is not concerned at any actual level with the place of the laity. The Decree affirms that the priest alone suffices for the Mass, the Easter Triduum, and the fullest celebration of the Mass. By not referencing the liturgical principle of full, active, and conscious participation by all the faithful in the Mass, as articulated in *Sacrosanctum Concilium*, at an operative level, it implies that the Mass is said *for the people* but not *with the people*. The Decree places the laity in a theologically obscure place. One must conclude that the physical presence of the laity in Catholic worship is not a constitutive theological presence. Answering this way, the Decree has dealt transactionally with the Mass and ignored any attempt to engage with the communion-ecclesiology theology of Pauline liturgy. It suggests that the Decree's operative theology lies elsewhere.

This Decree in a time of an international pandemic needs to be accepted as the carefully considered work of experts in liturgy and as the authoritative articulation of the Church's liturgical theology. We have no reason to doubt this. The Church issued the Decree as the guiding principle for the celebration of the Paschal Triduum, one of the Church's central liturgical rites. Nevertheless, it is concerning that the Decree's assessment of the place of the laity in the celebration of the Eucharist is minimal. In the context of the Paschal Triduum, the participation of lay-faithful was dealt with in one sentence: 'The faithful should be informed of the times of the celebration so that they can prayerfully unite themselves in their homes'. The physical presence of the laity is not required. For the laity, 'the means of live (not recorded) televisual or internet broadcasts are helpful'.

Given the context of Covid, this seems perfectly reasonable because the laity could not physically come to church. From this perspective, the Decree could be seen as consoling in an extraordinary time of confusion and danger if it were not for the underlying presumption that liturgy does not fundamentally include the laity. Because the Decree was written for bishops and priests, it makes no effort to explore active participation for the laity—which is essential to the Pauline liturgy—neither does it offer other means—other than looking on—by which the laity might celebrate the

Paschal days. The Decree simply ignores the principle of active participation in article seven of *Sacrosanctum Concilium*. It makes no effort to explore the active participation of the whole Church—head and members, ordained and lay, each in their proper order—as a constitutive element of the Easter Triduum and the Mass. It is illustrative of a clerical mindset that sees liturgy as an exclusively clerical action to which the lay faithful are not directly connected or required for sacramental or liturgical validity but only invited because liturgy is transacted by the priest.

Although the Decree was issued when public religious gatherings were prohibited, it does not offer the baptised faithful viable liturgical alternatives, nor does it counsel priests and bishops to share a eucharistic fast along with their parishioners. For example, it could have required bishops to create pastoral responses or given guidelines for one online paschal celebration in each diocese. It could have asked priests to experience the eucharistic fast or given instructions on the use of digital platforms and communion separated from the Mass.

The Decree ignores the nature of physical participation in the liturgy. It fails to comprehend that eucharistic participation includes the reception of the eucharistic elements—by the attending person (lay and cleric)—from the altar at the Mass at which they are present. Consequently, it does not mention either *Sacrosanctum Concilium* or the *General Instruction of the Roman Missal*'s reference to the reception of holy communion as the 'more perfect form of participation in the Mass by which the faithful after the Priest's communion, receive the Lord's Body from the same Sacrifice' as a constitutive element (GIRM13, SC55). The Decree also ignores the Council of Trent's admonition: 'at each Mass, the faithful should communicate not only by spiritual desire but also by sacramental reception of the Eucharist (*Doctrina de ss. Missae sacrificio*, C6, DS,1747). These references underscore the physical presence of all the baptised at the Eucharist. They emphasise the nature of shared consumption of the eucharistic elements by the assembly as the sign of eucharistic participation. They all prevent the nonsense of drive-up communion.

Sadly, the Decree does not reference the fundamental liturgical theology articulated in the GIRM, especially Chapter Three, Duties and Ministries in The Mass and Chapter Four, The Different Forms of Celebrating Mass. In these chapters, the place of the whole Body of Christ, laity, and clergy, together, is foundational:

> In the celebration of Mass, the faithful form a holy people, a people of God's own possession and a royal priesthood, so that they may give thanks to God and offer the unblemished sacrificial Victim not only by means of the hands of the Priest but also together with him and so that they may learn to offer their very selves.[1]

Chapter Four begins with the presumptive or ordinary form of the Mass celebrated with the faithful's participation.[2] This is followed by the rubrics for concelebrated masses. Then, last, the rubrics for masses at which only one minister participates, thus showing the hierarchy of meaning and practice. Mass celebrated by the priest alone presumes another lay minister or another person assists him. In number 254, the *General Instruction* makes this point explicit: 'Mass should not be celebrated without a minister or at least one of the faithful, except for a just and reasonable cause',[3] without further clarification. One can speculate that elderly and enfeebled clergy and those unjustly deprived of a community or liberty are intended here.

Canon Law contributes to the confusion. Canon 904:

> Remembering always that in the mystery of the eucharistic sacrifice the work of redemption is exercised continually, priests are to celebrate frequently; indeed, daily celebration is recommended earnestly since, even if the faithful cannot be present, it is the act of Christ and the Church in which priests fulfil their principal function.4

Canon 906 contradicts canon 904 where it states:

> Except for a just and reasonable cause, a priest is not to celebrate the eucharistic sacrifice without the participation of at least some member of the faithful.[5]

Here the principles of participation and just cause are conflicted; the operative principle appears to be that celebrating Mass is an act which 'fulfils' the priest's 'principal function'. This seems to underpin the Decree's approach. Many would argue that the pandemic provides a just and reasonable cause for priests to say Mass alone. But what is a just and reasonable legal cause is not necessarily a good and just theologically principle; the law is not a theological reality. Many would say a priest who is impeded from celebrating mass through age, infirmity, deprivation of liberty or deprived of public ministry fits this category. But does this category include a pandemic? Who justifies the cause and makes the response reasonable?

Unfortunately, by taking the legal framework, the General Instruction does not provide a theological rationale for celebrating Mass in the absence of the laity. A theological view places the praxis of the liturgy—the actual celebration—as a theological act and not a legal act. A liturgical-theological reading of the intimate relationship between what is symbolised and signified challenges Canon Law's 'just and reasonable cause' based on the 'work of redemption' being constantly 'exercised'. The canonical approach offers a weak soteriology based on a questionable understanding of the Paschal Mystery and an inadequate understanding of worship. This happens because it does not reference liturgical anamnesis.

Canon Law is caught because it does not fully understand the liturgy of God is primarily the work of Christ, the Priest—died, risen, and ascended—and that the Church's liturgy is its anamnesis or calling to mind of this. The liturgy— or Mass—of the Church is a corporate act of the baptised—head and members—in which, and for which—the priest's function is one of service. Presenting 'the principal function' of the priesthood as the cultic act, and the priest as its sacrificial surrogate, the Law, forgets that the priest fulfils the principal function of priesthood when he presides at sacraments *for and with* the baptised assembly and that he does not fulfil this principal function in private.

Presbyterorum Ordinis, the *Decree on the Pastoral Ministry and Life of Priests*, locates the priest's ministry within the 'apostolic proclamation of the Gospel'. Then it refers to the eucharistic link of the 'spiritual sacrifice of the faithful to the sacrifice of Christ'.[6] According to *Presbyterorum Ordinis*, the priest's function as the minister of

God's Word is the basis of his sacramental ministry and prior to his ministry of presiding at the Eucharist, 'the center of the assembly of the faithful'.[7] *Presbyterorum Ordinis*'s firm conviction is that the priest's primary ministry as minister of Word and sacraments is most fully expressed within the liturgy.[8] Thus, it is anomalous to suggest in Canon Law that celebrating the Mass without the people expresses union with Christ's priesthood.

Thus, a liturgical-theological view does not begin by reducing the Mass or the eucharistic celebration to the priest's function. Instead, it offers another hierarchy of relationships starting with (1) the relationship between the presences—Word, Sacrament, People, and Presider—and (2) the relationship between symbolisation and signification. The relationships between the presences and the symbols and signs are the building blocks of the interrelationship between all the participants in the act of liturgy and God. Relationships call for creative, active and conscious participation between the presences of Christ articulates in symbol and sign. They express the anamnetic relationship between the words spoken and the gifts received by the Church—the Body and Blood of Christ—in the Eucharist. This fuller expression of the liturgy and the Eucharist relies on the primary priesthood of Christ expressed liturgically in the ministry of the ordained priest and in the ministry of the baptised believer when both are present. A priest cannot proclaim the Gospel to empty pews; the community cannot receive the Eucharist communion via the internet. This theological hierarchy cannot be comprehended by law because of the nature of law itself. In short, a legal view is valid but stops short of being a theological one. Thus, the legal justification for saying Mass without an attending congregation is, of itself, insufficient. What makes the exception possible must be based on a theological rationale and not on the legal function of the priesthood.

Canons 904 and 906 enable priests to celebrate Mass alone by conflating function, personal spirituality, and piety. This creates a "theology of necessity" that is often a "theology of emotion" that justifies priestly functions. The implication is drawn that the Mass works as the continual theological necessity that keeps the work of redemption going as if God could forget the Paschal Mystery and its effects without it. Because the canonical construct lacks a nuanced reference to anamnesis, the implication is given that the relationship between the celebration of the Eucharist and the ministry of the priest is co-terminus for salvation: 'in the mystery of the eucharistic sacrifice the work of redemption is exercised continually, priests are to celebrate frequently'. Clearly, the celebration of the Mass does not remind God to save or make salvation present again as if redemption were conditional. The liturgical concept of anamnesis clarifies that the Eucharist is an act of remembrance that recalls what Jesus did and effectively makes it present again. This does not deny the sacrificial nature of the Mass or the real presence of Christ in the consecrated species of bread and wine. Instead, it clarifies that the function of the Mass—as the liturgy—is different from the function of the priesthood.

The legal presumption that the eucharistic celebration by the priest fulfils their principal function is the key to understanding the Decree and the proliferation of virtual masses. The functional gives meaning and form to the 'act of

Christ' as far as the law is concerned, and this approach is widespread. There is a sense that if the function of the Mass is not transacted, the work of redemption is not done, which borders on a type of fundamentalism. It suggests a fundamentalist understanding of the priest's function as the community's surrogate, the one who offers sacrifice for the community. This sort of view takes us back to the sacrificial, cultic priesthood that the Christian priesthood, in its original expression, shunned. In cultic sacrificial priesthoods, the effects of the sacrifice are measured positively in merit and satisfaction or negatively in damnation and sin. This approach objectifies the sacrifice and the priesthood. It robs the Eucharist of its symbolic ontology because it stops the symbol from becoming the transformative presence of Christ. Finally, it relies upon the priority of a clericalist mindset that necessarily eclipses the participation of the laity. The operative theology of the Mass could be summed up thus: the Mass is the work *of* the priest *for* the people but not *with* the people.

Why This Operative Theology?

One might ask why we still have such an operative theology present in the Church more than 50 years after the Second Vatican Council. The answer is multifaceted; the rejection of the Council; the slowing down of conciliar change during the pontificates of Popes John Paul II and Benedict XVI; the recruits to the priesthood; the drop in vocations; the loss of people from the Church; the growth of neo-traditionalist groups, and more besides.

From the point we can talk about a normative form of the Mass—*missa normativa* or *missa typica*—we see a single consistent norm among the enormous variety; namely, the Eucharist is the celebration of the whole baptismal assembly (bishop, clergy, and people). Despite enormous liturgical diversity, the history of Christian worship shows consistent agreement that the Eucharist is the worship paid to God by the baptised, the Mystical Body of Christ. Irrespective of disputes concerning the structure and rites of the eucharistic liturgy, episcopal authority, and the nature of God or Christ, one thing remains evident: the assembly of the faithful is the subject of the liturgy.

Over the centuries, in the West Church, the presence of the community became less and less necessary. From the early Middle Ages through to the mid-20th century, the function of the cultic priest was reasserted as the mediator on behalf of the people; effectively, the priest became the cultic surrogate. The Reformation and culture of Counter-Reformation Catholicism reinforced this thinking. It underpinned the practice of multiple masses by what came to be known as "massing priests". These priests prayed multiple masses each day for a stipend, assisted by a server or a small number of the laity. The misnomer "Private Mass" that described this activity also underscored the non-participation by the laity in the Mass. Along with the practice of numerous masses went the decline in the reception of holy communion by the laity. This reached its lowest point when church councils directed that the laity receive communion at least once each year to fulfil their obligation.

The form of Mass was essentially the same whether the priest prayed a solemn high Mass or a private one, as he was the only official voice. Eventually, many would mistakenly conclude that the server assisting the priest at Mass represented the community. Before the Vatican liturgical reform, a layman who read the epistle inside the sanctuary rails and a laywoman who read outside the sanctuary was not the official or only voice. For validity reasons, the priest still read the epistle at the altar in Latin as a function of his Mass.

Attending any form of the Mass in the years leading up to the Second Vatican Council was an experience of praying at "Father's Mass". According to Klemens Richter, this form was not prized in church documents and the broader literature. Richter comments that this medieval type of thinking had led to liturgical individualism and a static-objective conception of Eucharist and liturgy, where the priest gained grace for others and then dispensed it to them, irrespective of whether the person in question was present or not, or even believed or not. [9] However, this type of thinking is still operative in many parts of the Church.

Following the Second Vatican Council, the normative Mass (1970) became the Mass of the entire People of God, head, and members. The *messa cum populo* is the normative structure. In this form, the People of God gather around Christ to remember and give thanks for God's work of salvation. They participate in the work through anamnesis given as praise and thanksgiving before being sent back into the world to live like Christ. The active participation and con-celebration (*participatio actuosa* and *con-celebratio*) of the people required the rite of Mass to be revised 'in such a way that the intrinsic nature and purpose of its several parts, as well as the connection between them, maybe more clearly shown, and that devout and active participation by the faithful may be more easily achieved'(SC50). The participation of the assembly in the eucharistic celebration is described as a presence of Christ.

In March 2021, the Vatican Secretariat of State issued a new instruction limiting the practice of individual Masses at St Peter's Basilica. It caused an uproar among traditionalist clergy and communities in Rome,[10] a precursor to *Traditiones Custodes*. The Instruction placed stricter limits on the use of the 1962 Extraordinary Rite. Traditionalist priests, used to saying their daily private masses alone, saw this as a limitation on their rights as priests. They rejected the invitation to concelebrate. They did not want to participate in masses where concelebration is the norm, nor join in masses where laymen and women are lectors or cantors.

In June 2021, the archpriest of St Peter's Basilica, Cardinal Mauro Gambetti, issued an instruction pulling back some of the directives given in the March Instruction due to the mounting pressure from the culture of the "priest's mass". Gambetti gave greater concessions to those who want to celebrate masses on their own while reiterating that 'what is exceptional' should not 'become ordinary' and thereby distort 'the intentions and meaning of the Magisterium'. The need for this instruction and its aftermath indicates one cannot presume that Catholic clergy accept or even want laity at worship. It also indicates the entrenched culture of private masses and how hard it is to reform this culture.

Gambetti's references to *Sacrosanctum Concilium* are instructive: 'liturgical services are not private functions, but are celebrations of the Church, which is the sacrament of unity'; concelebration is 'to be preferred, so far as possible, to a celebration that is individual and quasi-private'; and the 'greatest fruit of the Eucharist is drawn from participation (clergy and laity) in the same action because it better expresses the mystery that is celebrated'. Clearly, the resistance to change is significant, and the theology of Vatican II is not the operative theology for many of his colleagues.

In the Mass, the Church comprehends herself as a eucharistic community—*communio*—through the liturgy and the shared consumption of the eucharistic meal. By effectively excluding the laity, the Decree has ignored the ancient tradition of the Church and her eucharistic ecclesiology and paid scant attention to the presumptive form of the Mass.

Placing the physical presence of the worshipping community as a secondary consideration, the Decree reduced the active, conscious participation of the baptised community to a theologically non-essential. Permitting the clergy to celebrate the Easter sacraments without the active participation of the baptised assembly has strengthened the role of the massing-priest over the gathering of the universal priesthood. It has reinforced that the celebration of the Eucharist is primarily, or exclusively, a clerical ministry *for* the laity but not *with* them.

The implications of this are important because one is left questioning if clergy and the Vatican dicastery for liturgy have failed to understand the liturgical renewal of the Second Vatican Council. Is the Decree an example of the resistance to the vision of Vatican II or an example of how space, place and presence are conceived in a narrow, clerical way?

---

[1] General Instruction of the Roman Missal (GIRM), Chapter III, n 95, in The Roman Missal, English Translation, Third

Typical Edition, Wellington, 2010, 33. Here after the General Instruction or GIRM.

2 GIRM, Chapter IV, 1, 115, 36.

3 GIRM Chapter IV, III, 254, 49.

4 Code of Canon Law [CCC], Latin–English Edition, New English Translation, Canon Law Society of America, Washington, DC 1999, canon 904, 295.

5CCC, canon 906, 296.

6 Presbyterorum Ordinis, Decree on the Pastoral Ministry and Life of Priests, 7 December 1965 in The Basic Sixteen Documents, Vatican II, Constitutions, Decrees, Declarations, A. Flannery, ed., (New York, Dublin: Costello Publishing and Dominican Publications,1996), 318ff. Hereafter PO.

7 PO., 325.

8 PO., 325.

9 See, Klemens Gemeinde im Herrenmahl. Zur Praxis der Meßfeier (Pastoralliturgische Reihe in Verbindung mit der Zeitschrift "Gottesdienst"). Einsiedeln/Freiburg i. Br. (1976).

10 The instruction allowed for masses in the basilica grottos for pilgrim groups and for the continued use of the 1962 missal at limited morning times in the Clementine Chapel.

PART THREE
VIRTUAL PRESENCE

Virtual Mass

Virtual masses became normative because they were (1) accessible, (2) easily transferred online, and (3) because they fitted the operative theology of worship for many Catholics. The availability of digital platforms enabled the already existing transactional, performative experience of Catholic liturgy to continue in the virtual environment. Live-streaming masses created the demand for more. This response, born of the need to keep in touch and show the Church is contemporary, exposed the unresolved tension in modern worship and pastoral practice, namely, the theological place and presence of the laity.

Parishioners, too, went viral in their search for masses. They commented on the quality or otherwise of the preaching, the emptiness of the church, the intimacy of a private chapel, and the presence or absence of other people. One parishioner remarked how wonderful it was to zoom in to masses in New Zealand on a weekday and to the United States on Sunday. Because of the time differences, she could zoom Mass before lunch or after the evening meal from the comfort of her couch. Many parishioners commented that they had landed in masses in another country by chance, remarking on the differences and similarities.

Priests writing enthusiastically of presiding over larger online congregations than usual and believers enthusing over watching Mass from their armchairs are not to be ignored. These experiences are also "liturgical" experiences. The experience of virtual worship has redefined the technological dimension of contemporary worship. It has reduced the need for physical gatherings of the Church and increased liturgical choice. As a result, liturgical theology must now deal with technology, physicality, choice, and virtuality as aspects or expectations of worship.

The technological dimension of liturgy came to the fore for me in an article published in *La Croix International* by Fr Michael Kelly SJ when he wrote:

> Today we face another challenge, and for the life of me, I can't see that a 'virtual' participation in the Eucharist is theologically any different to what happens at Eucharistic extravaganzas occurring at papal Masses across the world.1

Fr Kelly's article raised several critical points regarding virtual worship, liturgical memory (anamnesis), and liturgical presence. He contrasted viewing a papal Mass on a large screen from a distance with viewing it on a home television or computer monitor and asked what the difference is. Kelly also challenged readers to consider the nature of the future of communications and not prefer traditional, physical experiences of worship over newer technological ones. He wrote:

> Many, perhaps most commentators on the place of technology in such things as the celebration of the Eucharist are completely convinced that only the manner and methods we have employed to date are the only way for us to frame the questions before us— liturgy is about the physical, face to face gathering of a community; the Eucharist is the

privileged moment when a community is gathered by the Holy Spirit in the same place at the same time.[2]

Kelly described this reading as "fundamentalist". In his words, it ignores a worshipping community's 'context, circumstances and questions' and reflects 'an impoverished sense of what the technology available everywhere today actually aims to do'. He contends that technology had broken through the wall of 'the privileged moment' of the physical gathering and had reformed the way we celebrate Eucharist and the presumptions we bring to that experience.

In my response to his article, I attempted to show that "real" and "virtual" are distinct modes of communication, relying on a definition that defines virtual communications as having virtuality. I attempted to distinguish between virtual and other forms of presence using the computing distinction of virtual as "almost", "nearly", or "not completely there". My assessment and that of Mr Robert Mickens in his *Letters From Rome* were critiqued by Fr Flex Just, SJ. In his response to my article, Just identified a false dichotomy:

> now opposing "virtual" vs. "real," when the difference is actually between "virtual reality" and "physical reality." Both are "real," although in different ways. To avoid such false oppositions, we need greater terminological precision and philosophical nuance.'[3]

I had asked if the quality of my digital presence is precisely the same as my physical presence, and I maintained there is a qualitative difference between virtual presence and face-to-face presence that is necessary for liturgy. Fr Just agreed these two presences are not the same: 'they are not exactly the same; yet this does not mean that one type of "presence" is "real" while the other is "not real".'[4]

I had asked if the 'digital solution' is appropriate for the eucharistic celebration and concluded that this 'depends on how one understands reality, the virtual and presence' and on how one 'distinguishes "virtual reality" from "real reality" or "virtual presence" from "real presence"'. These distinctions were critical for me if the appropriateness of virtual presence for the celebration of the Eucharist was to be answered. It was at this point, Fr Just wrote, that I had slipped into the "false dichotomy" by mistakenly opposing "virtual" with "real" rather than 'virtual reality with physical reality', which are both '"real," although in different ways.'[5]

Digital communication platforms solve the problem of physical presence by providing virtual presence. They are designed to give a one-way-at-a-time form of communication.[6] Nevertheless, the question remained whether virtual presence provided technologically is sufficient for the celebration of the Eucharist. Suppose technology is the answer to the eucharistic dilemma. What is the essential characteristic of technology that enhances liturgy and eucharistic presence? If technology is the future, there is no longer any reason to privilege the 'physical, face to face gathering of a community…in the same place at the same time'.

The distinction I attempted to draw between virtual as "almost", "nearly", or "not completely there" was intended to draw attention to the qualitative nature of technological platforms. These platforms, by their nature, do not have "being-in-itself". They do not have their "own existence". Consequently, the virtual presence is insufficient and is not fit for worship. This lack of "essentialness" means that reality is incomplete when presented electronically or digitally. This incompleteness is an essential incompleteness. As such, its incompleteness lacks the essential dynamism required for liturgy.

It is a fine line to draw when a virtual or physical presence possesses a reality. But the question remains, are those realities equivalent? I was at this stage only talking about the presence of the people and not the Real Presence of the Eucharistic Species. I concluded that 'virtual and real are not equivalent' as evidenced in 'the adjectival requirement to describe one presence as virtual without describing the other as real'. At this point, I should have written virtual reality and physical reality to avoid the 'false dichotomy' I was trying hard to avoid. I wanted to distinguish the virtual and physical environments by contrasting the physical and virtual experiences. I used the wrong words.

Anamnesis and Liturgical Presence

Michael Kelly raised the question of anamnesis and liturgical presence when he wrote:

> What Vatican II called the 'source and summit of our faith' [is]…a virtual experience if ever there was one—the Eucharist. It is an exercise of our memories, which brings to mind every time it is celebrated, a meal shared by at most twenty or so people and refers us back to some things that occurred 2000 years ago. In relation to them and the events they recall, we are only virtually present— 'Do this in memory of me'. These

are actually ripe for transformation in a virtual age.[7]

Anamnesis[8] and epiclesis are the twin poles around which the narrative of our history of salvation moves. It is impossible to consider Christian sacramental liturgy's theological meaning and function without understanding them.[9] Anamnesis and epiclesis are the twin poles of the memorial of salvation history and its fulfilment. By mentioning one without the other, Kelly has aligned memory with virtuality. The essential relationship between anamnesis and epiclesis is memorial and invocation; this gives sacraments their liturgical framework of sanctification.

The anamnetic structure of Christian prayer is derived from the Jewish prayer forms of the *Berakoth* and *birkat ha-mazon*. Peter Fink reminds us of the original language, of zikkaron, "the original sense of remembrance". *Zikkaron* is not imagination, ordinary memory, or recall. Likewise, anamnesis, understood as *zikkaron*, enables us to enter the action—through memory—and participate in it in a proximate way.

Anamnesis can be understood analogously as "body-memory". If, for example, as a child, you experienced fear in a small, dark space and as an adult, you experienced the same fear, not only does your mind recall the fear, but so does your body. In this adult experience, you remember, and you experience yourself remembering. Your "body-memory" or anamnesis is not virtual; it is physical and proximate. Your body has remembered the event—with all its emotions—and transported you, via *zikkaron*, to the place of your fear. Thus, zikkaron memory is experiential. The zikkaron-memory-experience takes you into a more profound realm where meaning and experience meet in mysterion. *Zikkaron* is an experience of mysterion—something about which you know something, but not everything. In anamnesis, a more profound truth is explored. It is an ontological truth that is entirely proximate.

When individuals allow themselves to respond to an experiential-ontological reality, their body is "overtaken" by the experience of mysterion. German theologian Odo Casel described anamnesis expressing the unity between the originating event and every subsequent remembrance of that event. When applied to Christ, it is the actualising of Christ's sacrifice.[10]

Bernard Neunheuser's description of liturgical anamnesis situates the person, and zikkaron is pertinent:

> in the praises and blessings proper to the Old Testament berakah, [where] the person praying stands as it were in the presence of the saving act for which he praises the Lord, and he thereby acquires a share in it.[11]

When we add epiclesis or invocation to this dynamic understanding of anamnesis, not only do we gain a renewed appreciation of the place and function of the Holy Spirit in the sacramental and liturgical economy, but more importantly, we understand the relational proximity between *memoria* and presence. Thus, we can assert that the reality of God is proximate, not virtual. Critically, the memory and invocation that the Church uses to respond to God is the memory and invocation of the Father, Son, and Spirit. The Trinity's memory and invocation give the Church's remembrance and invocation its proximity.[12]

Consequently, liturgical memory enables us to see why liturgical presence is more than "just being there". Liturgical participation is more than "just watching" or even "just doing" something. There is an intentionality behind Christian worship that relies on more than "just" action, memory, or presence. It depends on the unity of action, memory, and presence as a proximate, coherent articulation of *zikkaron*. While this is not necessarily the case for the priest at his altar, it is the essential lack experienced by the layperson zooming in.

Anamnesis and epiclesis require physical proximity because memory and invocation are proximate realities, but the virtual environment works against them because 'Christ, in the power of the Holy Spirit' is no longer 'the source of the real communication between the liturgical assembly and the Father of all'.[13] Digital communication simply cannot communicate the intimacy required for Christian worship. It would be better to refrain from Mass than to practise it poorly.

The images of believers kneeling, standing, and sitting in front of their television screens, acting as if they were at Mass, are not instances of authentic liturgical participation. Unfortunately, inauthentic participation is more comforting for many than genuine truth: all who viewed a Mass online did not attend Mass or participate in the Eucharist. The clergy who celebrated alone said a private Mass. The fact that this was filmed or live streamed is irrelevant. The deeper problem is that we continue to treat worship as merely cultic action based on concepts of validity and lawfulness, not leitourgia.[14]

What we see too clearly is the operative theology of Mass is transactional. The nature of the transaction enables the Mass to become a virtual product. This transactional understanding of worship enables any priest to say Mass alone as his personal form of prayer. The transactional nature of worship supports those who want masses said for them and want to see the priest saying Mass. The transactional culture inherent in Catholic worship prevents liturgy from becoming transformative. Transactional thinking undermines the transformative interrelationships between action, memory, and presence essential for authentic liturgical participation. Transactional thinking inhibits believers from experiencing the Church as a sacrament and themselves as ministers of sacraments. Transformational theology offers a new vision. A vision remarked Karl Rahner that will be tremendously important for the consciousness of the Church.[15]

The Question of Presence

Presence, from the Latin, denotes something "being at hand" or proximate and physical. It implies being right there—relating to the body or its appearance, according to what exists in the physical world—as perceived by the senses and has a physical dimension. Virtual presence has the meaning of "almost", "nearly", or "not completely there". To be complete, it needs something additional to itself to make it complete.

A virtual environment generated by technology was enough for many people for Mass. Some theologians point out that being physically present in a church building during Mass does not ensure emotional presence to the liturgical rites, which is accurate but insufficient. So, do we gain a more profound sense of existence when we are physically present to each other? Up to now, that would have been the presumption of Catholic worship. When we are persuaded that virtual reality exists, it is no longer clear that physical presence is of greater value in worship than virtual presence. We cannot ignore the attraction of virtual worship as a means of worship when believers (clergy and laity) are persuaded by it.

When considering the nature of liturgical presence and trying to distinguish if virtual and physical are sufficient presences for worship, we need to consider that liturgy is an action that creates more than itself. German theologian and liturgist Romano Guardini called liturgy a doing or an activity: 'The path to liturgical life goes not merely through instruction, but rather, before all else, through doing'.[16] We could translate the intent of Guardini's sentence as: 'the way to liturgical life goes not via mere instruction, but rather through the act of doing of liturgy'. Or, again, 'the liturgical is not done primarily through knowledge but through activity'. The liturgical act, writes Guardini, is primary because it is where a person 'with all his or her creative power; a living (life-giving) consummation; a living (life-giving) experience, belief, and gaze' lives.[17]

For Guardini, the liturgy brings something into existence because it engages with an individual. It is a "doing" directed to another. For example, when lovers embrace, their love is given, one to the other, and their embrace is the symbol. The "doing" of love is internal first and then externalised in the embrace. The "doing" of the embrace brings the internal and external elements together in a mutual correspondence that is more than just an action. When we apply this type of structure to liturgy, we see that the relationship between the lover (God) and the beloved (Church) relies on a proximate relationship. This proximity is not a problem for the priest alone at his altar. Still, it is for the people looking on because they are not participating at the same level in the act of worship.

Worship's proximate relationship is expressed in posture, gesture, song, word, movement, ingestion, and more. Proximity includes talking, speaking, crying out, shouting, reading, and silence. It has singing, chanting, and drumming. It uses dancing, processions, standing, sitting, kneeling, walking, fetching, and carrying. Naturally, they differ from culture to culture and from place to place in their detail, but they create the "doing" of worship.

These proximate activities create the pattern of relationships within a single cultic act. Where physical proximity is ignored or broken, relationships that rely on it quickly become a shadow of their true self. Without proximate or physical relationality, the liturgy becomes a reduced form of communication and loses its dialogical character. Instead of being the dialogical or proximate form uniting the various activities within the cultic rite that relate the actors to each other, it becomes a monologue. If, for example, music and movement become too dominant, it is always at the expense of something else. The experience of proximity should—through posture, gesture, song, word, movement, ingestion, speaking, music, and movement—ground the experience of liturgical presence between the human, cultural, and divine participants.

The liturgy is a mode of ritual, dialogical communication. It is an experience that externalises its interior truth in a coherent unity. At the level of language, liturgical rites are disclosive, symbolic, and metaphorical. Ritual language is multi-dimensional in meaning and often given out of context to find a new context in the listener. It is a language that enables individuals to "see themselves" reflected in the metaphor or symbol. Metaphors are used dialogically to disclose something about God to the listener and give the listener a language to reveal themself to God.

Liturgical language is a performative language: "Lift up your hearts. We lift them up to the Lord!" The performative language calls for performative behaviours, "let us stand", says the Deacon to the assembly. It is more than just a stage direction; it is also an invitation to prayer through a specific posture.

All this points to liturgy being communication around two poles, as it were, the sender and the recipient. The sender speaks a message in a form the receiver can recognise; the receiver reworks this message into a medium they can understand. Therefore, communication relies equally on both the sender and recipient being active in their participation—both speaking and listening. Liturgy requires a mutual interaction, all of which builds unity:

> Liturgical services are not private functions but are celebrations of the church, which is "the sacrament of unity", namely, the people united and organized under their bishops. Therefore, liturgical services have to do with the whole body, the church, they make it visible and have effects on it. But they also touch individual members of the church in different ways, depending on ranks, roles, and levels of participation.[18]

Paradoxically, the Mass in a virtual environment is a private function even when it looks participative. Some argue it is not private because it is available to everyone. Many would say that full, conscious, and active participation is more attainable via a virtual Mass than in a church. Even some clergy have praised the larger number of people joining them online for Mass than ordinarily.

Nonetheless, I would suggest an online or virtual Mass is a private function because the Church is not present and proximate in her "ranks, roles".

---

1 Fr. Michael Kelly SJ, "Digital Catholicism. The Church needs to reflect deeply on 'virtual' ways to celebrate the faith", La Croix International, 13 April 2020.
2 Kelly, Digital Catholicism.
3 Felix Just, "Real Presence and Virtual Liturgies (Part I) A Response to Robert Mickens and J.P. Grayland", La Croix International, April 28, 2020, downloaded from: https://international.la-croix.com/news/religion/real-presence-and-virtual-liturgies-part-i/12261, 29 April 2020.
4 Just, Real Presence.
5 Just, Real Presence.
6 J.P. Grayland, "Liturgy is an act of the People of God, and they must be really present. A response to Michael Kelly SJ", La Croix International, April 17, 2020, https://international.la-croix.com/news/religion/liturgy-is-an-act-of-the-people-of-god-and-they-must-be-really-present/12200.
7 Grayland, "Liturgy is an act of the People of God".
8 Touto poieite eis ten emen anamnesin (1Cor. 11:24, 25, and Luke 22:19); hoskiseanpinete (1Cor. 11:25) concerning the cup. Hoc facite in meam commemorationem. See Sacred Congregation for Divine Worship: General Instruction of the Roman Missal4 (1975).
9 See, L. Bouyer: Eucharist (1966); E. Kilmartin: Christian Liturgy. Theology and Practice (1988); E. Schillebeeckx: The Eucharist (1968); E. Schillebeeckx: Church, The Human Story of God (1990); Schillebeeckx: Christ the Sacrament of Encounter with God 92-93; P. Fink: 'Theology of Eucharist' in P. Fink (ed.): The New Dictionary of Sacramental Worship (1990), 431-446.
10 O. Casel: Das Christliche Kultmysterium (1969), 79.

11 B. Neunheuser: "Odo Casel in Retrospect and Prospect", in Worship 50 (1976), 489-504, 496-497.

12 Christian zikkaron expresses the proximate anamnesis of Jesus, the Son of God, standing before the Father in the unity of the Spirit "remembering" the will of the Trinity for all creation to be saved. In this theological moment we—humans—receive God's anamnesis as our invitation to worship.

13 Kilmartin: Christian Liturgy 4.

14 In terms of canonical validity, one cannot say that a cleric saying mass on his own is not rendering anamnesis and epiclesis. What one can say is that this level of understanding is insufficient.

15 K. Rahner: "Das neue Bild der Kirche", in Schriften zur Theologie 8 (1968), 338.

16 Der Weg zu liturgischem Leben geht eben nicht durch blosse Belehrung, sondern er geht vor allem durch das Tun. Romano Guardini, Von heiligen Zeichen, 8.9.

17 Tun is etwas Elementares, in dem der ganze Mensch stehen muß, mit seinen schaffenden Kräften; ein lebendiges Vollziehen muß es sein; ein lebendiges Erfahren, Auffassung, Schauen. Guardini, Von heiligen Zeichen, 8.9.

18 SC 26, 128.

PART FOUR

TECHNOLOGY, AND

PRESENCE

Technology and Liturgy?

Fr Kelly's concern that discussion 'on technology and the Eucharist…misses the point about the purpose of the technology' is genuine. He rightly rejects the 'one-way communication that induces passivity' as the 'technology for voyeurs', which was the norm for most using virtual masses. The 'technology of voyeurs' is related to the transactional form and operational theology, not the technology itself. Online environments create passive audiences because the technology does not allow participants to interact except in a controlled and linear fashion. Participants cannot all talk at the same time.

Our communication forms are changing. The high uptake of digital worship during Covid reflects the equally high uptake of digital family gatherings. Virtual masses represent a mirroring of contemporary social connection and a transition towards it. Importantly, it is the worshippers who have innovated. Thus, Kelly is right to see a significant change in our liturgical communications structures and a movement towards digital Catholicism. This begs the question of a theology of technology and digital participation in a globalised, technological Catholicism.

In his article Kelly asks what we are learning through the restrictions on eucharistic gathering and concludes 'we are being forced to face a lot of things we either haven't had the time to consider or, more to the point, we haven't wanted to face'. He is entirely correct that we face issues like the shortage of priests. In the context of this book, I would suggest the biggest, unstated challenge is our own operative theological culture of Mass as a transactional, performative, clerical action. Kelly implies that if the clergy were better able to use technology, they could improve one-way communication. We saw attempts at two-way communion where priests and laity used technology to include others in liturgical elements by sharing their screens. Unfortunately, this was not the norm, and I think one comes to two inescapable conclusions. First, the clergy generally lacks the skills to use digital platforms, and second, many are comfortable with passivity in their attending audience.

In his article, Kelly asks what we are learning through the restrictions on eucharistic gathering and concludes 'we are being forced to face a lot of things we either haven't had the time to consider or, more to the point, we haven't wanted to face'. Thus, Kelly's point is not lost on me. I acknowledge the lack of clergy already drives the loss of eucharistic worship in many parts of the world. I also acknowledge the seeming consolation of virtual masses for many. Nonetheless, I disagree that digital worship is the way forward because it contradicts the fundamental nature of liturgy and begs another question: when is prayer not liturgy?

Fr Ricky Manalo[1] writes of the consolation of virtual masses:

> While livestreamed Masses are not intended to replace our regular Sunday gatherings in churches, they remain a valuable form of connecting, particularly to our homebound members, ministerial outreach, and evangelisation.[2]

He promotes the use of "intentional interactive liturgy" over the "liturgy-as-is" model as "ways of connecting". These are a valuable way of connecting but not valuable in themselves as worship. In the former, the intention of interactivity drives the liturgical experience, while in the second, it is more of a business as usual approach, with the emphasis mainly on the priest. In the intentional interactive liturgy, 'the liturgical ministers acknowledge the presence of online worshippers and offer support for all to participate better':

> Livestreamed Masses and interactive websites that offer more than digital information, as well as, Liturgy of the Hours, quality preaching and diverse music have attracted new "online parishioners" who live beyond diocesan boundaries to experience a particular parish. Collectively, online worship has redefined "destination parishes," provided unexpected flexibility for work schedules, relief for parents struggling with young children and infants and invited a myriad of people to worship in new ways.[3]

Although this does not provide participation as intended by *Sacrosanctum Concilium*, he writes, it does provide a form of pastoral care. While this is true, there are issues here. Unfortunately, Manalo does not tackle the critical question of what defines liturgy when it is more than just a pastoral outreach. He quotes Robert Taft's insight on the givenness of liturgy that brings the Church together but does not apply this insight to the fundamental distinctions between the experience of "togetherness" in the online environment and the experience of togetherness in the physical environment. He does not contrast what is received in the virtual environment with what is received in the physical environment, asking if these are qualitatively different because of their environments. The concept of the "destination parish" and the real motivation of an "online parishioner" who is even more detached from their local reality than they might have been before Covid are not explored.

The experience of Mass for the priest—in either the online or physical environment—is either the complete or greater experience of immediacy. All the "components" of presiding, praying, reading, listening, speaking, the eucharistic prayer, consuming the eucharistic elements are one for him and available to him. They are united and immediate. It is not the case for the online viewer. Even in an intentional interactive liturgy where an individual participates through reading a scripture text, saying a prayer, or giving a homily, the experience is only immediate and proximate to the speaker. It is a "zoomed-in" participation.

Manalo's reference to Andrew Ciferni's notion of the "now" of the liturgy avoids the critical issue: the separation of the "now" of the virtual participant from the "now" of the virtual priest. While each "now" *is* (singular), each is also plural. Although each "now" may be contemporaneous in space and time—depending on the time zone—they are not a single entity with each other. Thus, they are not one because they do not share the "nowness" of being or *sein*. I suspect the original context of Ciferni's comment must have been the "now" of the physically gathered community, not the digital community.

The clarity for Manalo's position comes in the example he gives from his homeland and how the extension of the liturgical space outside the church building creates the experience of the "overflow congregation". In this, he reflects Kelly's argument concerning papal masses:

> In the Philippines, television sets are placed outside the front entrance of churches, since most churches are filled to capacity. In many ways, livestreamed Mass is an extension of these practices; in many other ways, it is not the worshipful experience. Yet a consistent dynamic in these overflow scenarios is that while spatial variations may differ, everyone is connected to the one shared celebration of the liturgy. Online worshipers no doubt feel the difference between what is taking place in front of the camera and their experience at home, but given the pandemic context, many remain appreciative that all of us are somehow worshipping together.[4]

Herein lies the most explicit justification of the virtual Mass. The overflow experience is the key to using virtual masses in many countries, especially where "overflow" is normative. The congregation's presence inside the physical building praying the Mass includes those outside participating from the sidewalk. Where this is the norm, one can understand why the virtual Mass is less problematic and more prolific, given the normative experience and expectation of overflow—people are just "outside the church". Many are grateful that something is happening and consoled by it because they realise they couldn't have gotten inside even if they had wanted to. Overflow predisposes us to online masses. The catch is this: there are still people inside when I am in the overflow congregation. Although I am connected through the physical presence of others to the action of the liturgy inside the packed church, I am still on the pavement. My connection is proximate in a secondary way.

Digital technology like Zoom is not designed for overflow but inclusion. It offers us huge advantages for online learning, business meetings, team discussions and family conversations. Nevertheless, we also know—experientially—that being "virtually present" in a virtual classroom or meeting is substantially different from being physically present, even in an overflow situation. When I am standing outside a packed church in the overflow congregation, I am experientially not in a virtual environment. I am standing, physically and proximate to the action, probably hearing it, even if my seeing is mediated via a television.

The great value of digital platforms is how they link people who cannot be physically present to each other. The presence is digital through using VOIP and video cards; this is digital presence. In this unique environment, our communication is not immediate. Neither is it simultaneous—we cannot all speak at once and be understood. While I can see and hear others, my seeing and hearing have no immediacy of listening, seeing, hearing, talking.

When I communicate virtually, I inhabit two environments. First, the physical environment where my body experiences the touch of the chair, the light through the window, and the feel of the coffee cup. This experience is not shared in the virtual environment. I am virtually available to others but not present to them. Although I can see the other participants and talk to them, I can also send emails to people not in the meeting, take other calls and mute the meeting when it suits me. I can do this because the meeting participants do not encounter each other through the immediacy of the senses and do not share the same physical reality.

When I enter a physical environment, I have one reality. The place itself is filled with people. There is immediacy or proximity. In that place, I have a sensate encounter with others through their and my physical presence. My reality is sensate, and my conversations can be multiple. My experience of the existence of others to me, and me to them, is immediate. In this physical meeting, the presence is wholistic. In a physical environment, all participants can speak simultaneously, unlike in a virtual one where only one person can speak at a time. The interaction of people talking at once in a physical environment we call a conversation but people speaking simultaneously in a digital environment is just noise. In the physical world, audio (I hear) and video (I see) are one and not separated channels of data.

Fr Manalo's observation indicates a valuable but implicit distinction that should be attended to by those using video technology in a liturgical environment. The distinction between using digital media *during* the liturgy to connect those who cannot or would not be physically present (people in hospital or the overflow congregation) and using it *for* sacramental worship when no one is physically present. The distinction can be seen in televising an event like a Royal Wedding. With an active, proximate congregation present at the wedding, the online audience comprises millions of people who would never ordinarily be present. Technology is used *during* the wedding, not *for* it. Here, the overflow principle is at play.

The intention is to celebrate the marriage with the physically present community and only—by implication—with the online audience. The overflow concept works with an already physically present proximate community. The intention of using the technology is not to make the experience of watching the wedding on television the same as physically being there, at any level beyond the romantic, irrespective of what television commentators might say.

This intention respects the qualitative difference between being there and looking on; the wedding is celebrated with the television audience only in a secondary way. This defines the difference between using technology *during* Mass from using technology *for* Mass.

Liturgy requires a particular type of active participation. The normative liturgical arts of movement, symbol, music, and posture are forms of liturgical participation, and each contributes to it. Because a virtual environment cannot replicate this, it cannot mediate the liturgy's immanent and transcendent elements. Not being able to sing, pray, and receive the sacramental elements together are signs of a deficiency. The deficiency communicates itself as a lack. Because virtual media cannot "communicate" the mysterion at the heart of the eucharistic liturgy, it is only apparently pastoral and only apparently consoling.

In *The Christian Commitment. Essays in Pastoral Theology* Karl Rahner, one of the most eminent theologians of the 20th century, addresses the televised Mass.[5] The question before him is should a Mass, at which an assembly is present, be televised? Rahner makes several noteworthy points. First, he asks, 'is it right for the…camera to see' what the believing Christian sees and celebrates in the Mass? Rahner points out that seeing is the same physical action for everyone; seeing is also an action with meaning. He asks, "do I have the right to see this" and, "do I have the right to show this"[6] as an intimate act of human lovemaking? Is an action of this magnitude too personal, intimate, and holy to be seen vicariously? Is the Mass too intimate an exchange between the believer, the Church, and God to be available to everyone on the internet?

Rahner concludes the Mass is an intimate act of vision because it is 'an act of personal love, the adoration of God.' To make the point, he refers to the *disciplina arcani* or sacred discipline of things hidden from view and given only to initiates. The act of worship—the Mass—holds its *disciplina arcani* in a proximate relationship of intimacy that is understood, loved, and participated in only by initiates. He gives the example of people laughing throughout the ceremony creating cardinals, and sitting with their sandwiches watching Mass.

Next, Rahner talks of a 'metaphysical sense of modesty that protects the personal centre' of the celebrated truth. The Mass exists on many different levels. Our entrée into the sacrament is via the ritual that uses a vocabulary of signs, symbols, postures, and gestures. These possess both an individual meaning and, together, shared meaning. The ritual vocabulary is not arbitrary; it relies on intimacy or affinity with the vocabulary to participate. Where intimacy with the ritual vocabulary is lost, the ability to relate to the ritual beyond the merely transactional is too.

In rejecting the televised Mass, Rahner makes two magisterial comments applicable to our consideration:

> The Mass is thus necessarily and essentially the embodiment of the most intimate religious acts of which any man is capable. But these acts...are subject to the dictates of metaphysical modesty. It would be shameless in the highest decree to perform

them in the sight of any and everyone's indifferent curiosity.[7]

An intimate religious act is not a product to keep people happy by giving them something to watch, as we sit children in front of the television to keep them occupied. Rahner warns that some people will not like his point because custom has framed and formed their approach to the sacred and 'reduced this sense of modesty'. The celebration of the Eucharistic requires of those attending the capacity to worship and to share ritually.

Rahner points out that those who televise—in our case, live stream—masses have no control over where the images end up, who watches them and how they are used. Like pornography, YouTube masses exist in cyberspace as a sacred moment, out of context for the anonymous users' pleasure or otherwise. Online and live-streamed masses expose the sacred texts and symbols to everyone irrespective of their capacity to understand and their capability to give worship— this is not the same for a Mass televised from a hospital chapel to a patient's bed in a closed system. In the open cyber world, one can admit anyone into the 'innermost mystery of religion' and have no control over how this intimate act between God and community is experienced.

More problematic are the justifications for virtual masses that separate the cultic and the sacramental and the ontological and the experiential. Rahner writes:

> If then, there is in religion and in Christianity anything at all that is so sacred as to belong within a space set apart from the profane world, namely the temple formed by the communion of saints, then that thing is the most central cult-action of the Church, the

mystery of the holy Mass. Not only because it is the bodily performance of the most personal of all acts on the part of the faithful, such as naturally belongs with the sphere of personal modesty; but also because the Mass is in itself the bodily manifestation of the grace of God, the presence of the Son of God and his Cross: the Holy Thing which, at the very least, demands not to be proffered to just everybody by the person at whose disposal it is placed.[8]

Based on the experience of saying Mass in the virtual environment will come the justification of virtual masses—an argument from practice to principle. Just because you can say Mass online in the virtual environment is not a good enough reason to do it. Rahner reminds his readers one cannot argue from: 'what happens in practice to what is legitimate in principle, from what is contingence to what is essence'. The ends do not justify the means.

Liturgy is sacred because it is the Church's active, participative response to the revelation of God. Liturgy is not a product of the Church's life for the cyber world; it cannot be password protected. The liturgy presumes the use of symbols and signs that can be "received" by the participants.

My issue is not with the technology but with the operative, transactional theology that drove our use of it. I am convinced that liturgy requires a proximate physical relationship between the participants for which digital or virtual platforms are insufficient. People know this to be true when they say the virtual Mass "is not the same as the real thing". Despite this, priests and people continue using an artificial form and expect it to be life-giving.

Sacred Physical, Proximate Presence

The effect or fruitfulness of the Eucharist is related to the symbolic meaning and enactment of the eucharistic ritual. The fruitfulness of the Eucharist is mainly spoken of in terms of validity. Validity relies on the priest's consecratory power (ordination), correct disposition (being in a state of grace), intention (do as the Church does), and attention to what he is doing.

In this paradigm, the Mass belongs to the context of the priest's power. Individuals are the potential recipients of communion and Grace when all other conditions are met (baptised, age of reason, in a state of Grace, disposition) for the correct celebration of the Eucharist. For both laity and clergy, the eucharistic fast is required.[9] Apart from the requirements of disposition, intention, and permission, there are legal requirements that the "material" of bread and wine must be correct—real, unleavened, bread and grape-based wine. Finally, there is the requirement that the "form" of words used in the consecratory prayer is correct and used as given.

These considerations focus on the individuals' lawful, valid, and proper disposition, but there is another way to view sacramental worship and the Eucharist.

While not calling the role of the ordained into question, my focus is to present the celebration of the Eucharist as more than a sum of its validity and more than just an act of the ordained. Liturgy celebrates the singular 'paschal banquet in which Christ is received, the mind is filled with grace, and a pledge of future glory is given for us'.[10] In the liturgical act, using symbols and signs comprehensible to the senses, all the baptised participate according to their ministry. In what follows, I am setting to one side the canonical requirements of validity to focus on how and why the liturgical act is the source and high point of the whole Christian life because it is the gathering of the baptised. I rely on contemporary sacramental theology's understanding of the communication structure of sacramental mediation as a dialogue between persons as articulated in *Sacrosanctum Concilium* 5–11. The frame of the liturgy is the personal encounter between the healing, holy God and the people who are healed and made holy, in God.

In this dialogue between the healer and the healed, the Eucharist's inner meaning is revealed through verbal and non-verbal symbols. These are articulated in rituals and used in rites. Signs and symbols accessible to the senses that cause Grace and require thanksgiving, *sacramenta significando causant gratiam.*[11] This axiom expresses the critical relationship between a symbol and its ritualisation in words and actions in worship. The relationship between ritualisation and symbol reveals the liturgy as both ground and principle of theology.

The relationship between the physical and the symbolic is critical to ritual. Symbolic awareness and physical experience marked the Patristic Church's understanding of liturgy, weakened in the Western Church throughout the Middle Ages but revived throughout the 20th century. The sacred symbol is the liturgy itself. Liturgy's sacramental character is expressed in words, gestures, and physical elements; the *signum rememorativum* (remembrance or inspiration). The articulation of sacramental grace is the *signum demonstrativum* (demonstration or nowness). Remembrance and nowness combine to express the eschatological completion of life with and in God; thus, liturgy becomes a *signum prognosticum* (what is foreshadowed). Breaking these symbols apart reduces the liturgy to either mere symbolisation or ritualism. Consequently, every act of liturgy is a meeting with God, and it is always grace-filled.

The *signum rememorativum,* *signum demonstrativum,* and *signum prognosticum* live in a foundational relationship. The Church—Christ's mystical body—celebrates this relationship in the liturgy of the sacraments as the body of believers. In the Eucharist, they receive the Body and Blood of Christ, offered with the priest at the altar, and seek and experience a deeper union with God in Christ:

> The church, therefore, spares no effort in trying to ensure that, when present at this mystery of faith, Christian believers should not be there as strangers or silent spectators. On the contrary, having a good grasp of it through the rites and prayers, they should take part in the sacred action, actively, fully aware, and devoutly. They should be formed by God's word and be nourished at the table of the Lord's body. They should give thanks to God. Offering the immaculate victim, not only through the hands of the priest by also together with him, they should learn to offer themselves. Through Christ, the Mediator, they should be drawn day by day into ever more perfect union with God and each other, so that finally God may be all in all.12

The Church is present or proximate because the believer is not a spectator. The believer takes part consciously, actively, fully aware, and devotedly and is the recipient of both Word and Sacrament. Believers participate with the presider in the sacred offering of which Christ is the Priest. Through Christ's priesthood, the believer comes into a relationship with God. Here is the basis of the ecclesial-communion character of the Pauline liturgy. Underpinning this is the covenantal theology of the institution of the Eucharist, witnessed to in the New Testament: the blood covenant (Mk 14:22l; Mt 26:28) and the new covenant in Jesus' blood (1Cor 11:25; Lk 22:20).

Liturgy is an epiphany! The relationship between the Mystical Body of Christ and the person of Christ established in Christian initiation forms the Church. It is given symbolic form in the reception of holy communion, which is the sign of *communio* with Christ himself in and through his Body, the Church. The epiphany of active participation is the reception of communion by all the baptised. This is 'the more perfect form of participation in the Mass whereby the faithful, after the priest's communion, receive the Lord's body from the same sacrifice, is warmly recommended'.[13] The reception of communion by the entire assembly is necessary for two reasons. First, the Eucharist achieves its goal, as *actio*, in the delight of the Body of Christ eating and drinking in *communio* with Christ, under this sign of bread and wine (Body and Blood). The is the corporeal, real presence. Second, as the institution of Christ himself as food and covenant offered, blessed, broken, and given, the Eucharist is the liturgical "self-actualisation" of the Church as the Mystical Body of Christ. The people of the new covenant, in all its clarity, is revealed to itself when, as the Mystical Body of Christ, they receive the Body and Blood of their Lord.

Thus, Eucharist as *convivium paschale*, the new covenant in Christ's blood. The reception of holy communion is the sacramental completion of the prayer of faith made to God in Christ, with the

Holy Spirit—the fullest expression and experience of Christ, the high priest:

> At the last supper, on the night he was betrayed, our Savior instituted the eucharistic sacrifice of his body and blood. This he did in order to perpetuate the sacrifice of the cross throughout the ages until he should come again, and so to entrust to this beloved spouse, the Church, a memorial of his death and resurrection: a sacrament of love, a sign of unity, a bond of charity, "a paschal banquet in which Christ is received, the mind is filled with grace, and a pledge of future glory is given for us".[14]

---

1 "At the Digital Banquet of the Lord: Part One: A Primer on Livestreamed Mass",," Pastoral Music (special edition, Dec. 9, 2020). https://npm.org/wp-content/uploads/Ricky-Manalo_At-the-Digital-Banquet-of-the-Lord_Full.pdf), retrieved 13 May 2021.

2 Manalo, At the Digital Banquet, 1.

3 Manalo, At the Digital Banquet, 2.

4 Manalo, At the Digital Banquet, 3.

5 Karl Rahner, The Christian Commitment. Essays in Pastoral Theology, (trans.) Cecily Hastings, (Sheed and Ward, New York), 1963.

6 Rahner, The Christian Commitment, 208.

7 Rahner, The Christian Commitment, 210.

8 Rahner, The Christian Commitment, 212-213.

9 See Canons 900 to 930 of the 1983 Code of Canon Law, 295-301.

10 SC., 47, 134-5.

11 See SC., 7.

12 SC., 48, 135.

13 SC., 55, 136-7.

14 SC., 47, 134-5.

Active Participation

ctive Participation (*actuosa, plena et conscia participatio*) defines Pauline liturgical praxis and thinking. Active participation has an inner and an outer expression. The inner expression is in presence and silence and the external manifestations in listening, singing, and reciting, bringing gifts to the Table, and, ultimately, through sharing the communion of the Body and Blood of the Lord. In both its inner and outer expressions, liturgy is more than doing something about being a people. Because active participation expresses the reality of the liturgical assembly as the subject of the liturgy, it put an end to the pastoral and ritual clericalism that had marked the Mass and popular Eucharistic devotion since the Middle Ages.

The Pauline reform of the Second Vatican Council intentionally united the liturgical prayer of the priest and assembly in one interwoven prayer where believers do not go to hear the priest say his Mass while they pray their prayers in parallel. The clergy and laity pray together in one hierarchical body in the Pauline liturgy. Active participation is the simple and powerful organizational idea that frames this action. In this context, *Sacrosanctum Concilium* 10 reminds us that while to 'praise to God in the midst of his church, to take part in the sacrifice and to eat the Lord's supper', is the summit of the church's activity and number 12 reminds us that the Mass is not the only liturgical activity of the Church.[1]

Based on the principle of active participation, the liturgical books tell us that the sacramental rites should be 'celebrated in common, with the faithful present and actively participating.' This is true for all the sacraments, especially the Mass, which 'should as far as possible be celebrated in that way [physically presence] rather than by an individual and quasi-privately'.[2] The liturgical experience is intended to be a communal, physical, proximate experience of a body of believers, exercising their various ministries within a shared liturgical expression.

Ontologically, the liturgy expresses the authentic leitourgia of redemption. Where the experiential and ontological elements of the Eucharist are separated from the ritual celebration, the Eucharist becomes transactional. It is something done by someone for some gain. Transactional theology forgets the ontological-experiential relationship of the four presences of Christ established in *Sacrosanctum Concilium*.[3] The separation of the experiential from the ontological turns the Mass into magic. When the experience is not immediate, proximate, and experiential, worship becomes idolatrous because the cult of worship (rites and actions) become prized in itself. Where this is true, God is no longer the one who initiates and completes worship but is *God-a-prey-to-our-humanity*.

The experiential element demands we understand that our human participation in the sacramental action is an essential element that operates in us and not just on us. The experiential aspect of the celebration and reception of the Eucharist is not a purely cognitive experience. It is an experience of taste, touch, movement, reception, and eating. It is a multi-sided reality no one ever fully comprehends. The rites celebrate and proclaim God's deeper, more profound presence and action in the world; the ontological dimension brings us to contemplate the Paschal Mystery.

The ontological dimension of the Paschal Mystery reveals the presence of God and frames the nature of salvation. We are taken deeper into the "experience" of ontology (being) through the liturgical rites. The rites take us from the pool's shallow end towards the middle and eventually to its deepest end. They facilitate an experience beyond ritual that is intimate, human, and divine.

Across the pool, especially at the deepest end, there is a sense of being in ontic unity, beyond knowing, while being known, a place where the divine and the human are united. The ontological dimension ensures that we do not treat the Eucharist, God, salvation, and sacraments as things to be grasped and the priesthood as a purely cultic function. They are not subjective experiences that memorialise God or the Paschal Mystery for one's own benefit. They are not one's private possession or experience because they belong, ultimately, to God, who is intimately present.

The ontology of the celebration of the Eucharist and the other sacraments is a genuine re-presentation of the Paschal Mystery in sacramental form, using liturgical rituals. The liturgy expresses the ontological reality of God's authentic leitourgia of redemption in symbolic form. The ontological dimension prevents us from approaching the sacraments as personal possessions. It also stops us from approaching worshipping as a purely anthropological action.

The double dimension of ontology and experience stops us from exploiting the sacramental system as a religious production line that provides sacramental mediation for personal holiness. When the experiential-ontological relationship is broken, a pervasive individualism grows and develops a privatised, narcissistic approach to sacraments. It nurtures a "me and Jesus" mentality that thwarts eucharistic communion because it denies the communal dimension of salvation.

Breaking the experiential-ontological relationship creates the Harry Potter school of the liturgy where everything becomes magic. Everything is apparent in the Harry Potter liturgy school, but nothing is proximate. The experience is always apparent; one is apparently in communion, apparently at Mass, apparently worshipping but in fact, one is not because the foundation ground for this is not present. Where this is true, everything becomes a substitute for something else; thus, Spiritual Communion becomes the substitute for Holy Communion. The notion of eating is spiritualised to the point that it makes no sense ontologically or experientially. There is no communion with the Eucharistic sacrifice through its meal. Everything relies on a surrogate.

Magic shuns a proximate, physical connection between the ontological and experiential because magic relies on their separation. Magic is at play when priests declare they can simultaneously speak the words of epiclesis and institution over their bread and wine and—virtually—over the bread and wine of their online viewers. The separation of the experiential—the priest and the online viewer—should clarify what we are doing is magic. If not, the notion that the bread and wine are ontologically changed via telephonic links or a spiritual agency should convince us we are dealing with magic! We are dealing with magic in both examples because the foundational action is a deception of the senses. What is apparent has no reality.

No less problematic, but for other reasons, is the approach taken by priests when they have invited the online participants to pray the epiclesis and institution narrative with him over the bread and wine in front of them. While it is more authentic because it comes the closest to proximate truth and the authentic experience, there is still an element of magic. It is more authentic because it does not ape the Eucharist and does not present spiritual communion as realistic participation. But it fails to hold the ontological and experiential together because it excludes—at the moment— the ontology of the ministerial priesthood and the experience of liturgical presiders.

It is a more authentic sign because the prayer is said over proximate bread and wine in a physical setting for people who are proximate and will physically ingest. But, because the ministry of presiding is not present, the four presences of Sacrosanctum Concilium are not fully actualised.

Thus, it is problematic because it infers a private type of Eucharist because the eucharistic prayer is not with, for, and among the community of believers, who all receive from the same table and are united with the bishop and through him with the universal church. Instead, the eucharistic prayer becomes the prayer of groups or individuals who pray it simultaneously but not together as a single community, with their presider.

---

1 SC., 10, 122 and SC., 12,123
2 SC., 27, 128.
3 SC., 7, 120.

PART FIVE

MEDIATED

SACRAMENTS

Exceptional Times

In exceptional times, we turn to exceptional solutions or create them. The focus has been the online Mass and the celebration of the Eucharist, but this is not the only sacrament impacted by Covid-19. I would like to consider two other sacraments that believers have requested and not been able to receive, namely the sacrament of reconciliation and penance and the sacrament of the sick. Could the mediation of these sacraments be given exceptional forms?

Reconciliation and Penance

Covid has heavily impacted the sacrament of reconciliation. Believers have asked if a telephone confession and reconciliation is a valid form of the sacrament. Those who accept this form argue there is no qualitative difference between a disembodied penitent speaking from behind a confessional screen and a disembodied voice on the telephone. Those who say no reference their answers to the transportability of the priest's absolution down a telephone line, not the penitent's need or intention. A similar argument for virtual masses. The rationale goes: reconciliation is a sacrament that doesn't require physical mediation as an essential element. Thus, it could be celebrated via the phone because it is possible to celebrate it without the physical imposition of hands.

Those who argue that a telephone confession is qualitatively different from a virtual Mass because the person "is more immediately present" on the phone than they are watching Mass speak of a different "type" of mediation. The argument goes: it is more reasonable to say a person hearing the words of absolution over the phone (mediated to) is more engaged than someone hearing the words of Epiclesis and Institution over the bread and wine in a virtual Mass. Still, others hold all our sacraments are caught in the impediment of non-physical relationality, and we should leave them until we can celebrate them as they are intended to be celebrated.

Anointing of the Sick

Some have argued—before Covid and during it— for an exceptional form of the anointing of the sick a layperson can give in a hospital or home. One iteration is when the oil is blessed by the layperson and administered as the priest speaks the formula of anointing over the phone. Such innovations are dismissed based on the relationship between forgiveness of sin and the anointing as a reconciling sacrament that only an ordained priest or bishop can administer; Grace is not mediated telephonically.

Those who argue for lay anointing justify it on the basis that one believer is "ministered to" by another "in the name and service of the Lord," which they argue is consistent with the essence of mediation at the heart of our sacramental system. Referring back to the Letter of James, they say that the anointing is less about the elders who anoint and more about being anointed in the name and the power of Christ. The effect of anointing is not reliant on the person who administers it but on the prayer of faith that underpins it because the sacrament is not magic. The history of the anointing of the Sick or unction is a treasure of innovation and exceptions worth considering.

Early historical evidence shows that people brought oil to be blessed at the end of the Eucharistic Prayer and took this home to drink or anoint themselves or be anointed by another. Pope Innocent I's (402-417) letter to Decentius, Bishop of Eugubium, in 416, refers to the Letter of James and the anointing. Innocent writes: 'There is no doubt that this text must be received or understood of the sick faithful, who may be [lawfully] anointed with the holy oil of chrism, which, having been blessed by the bishop, it is permitted not only to priests but to all Christians to use for anointing in their own need or that of their families.'

Innocent explains 'this unction may not be given to penitents'—those undergoing a canonical penance—because it is a sacrament (quia genus sacramenti est). The rationale for this is simple: a sacrament cannot be given to someone to whom all the other sacraments, particularly the Eucharist, are denied. Clearly, one cannot say with absolute certainty that Innocent was defining a sacrament in the strictest terms, even when he refers to the relationship between anointing and the reception of the Eucharist. Based on James's letter, Innocent clarifies the Roman custom: the anointing given to the sick faithful who were not undergoing a canonical penance. His reference to bishops explains they can administer the anointing, and it belongs to their 'office…to consecrate the chrism'. The anointing can be given by priests, bishops, and laypeople, with oil blessed by the bishop. Caesarius of Arles is another witness who suggests laypeople were permitted to anoint themselves and household members with the oil consecrated by the bishop. Whether this anointing was identical with the Letter of James or a devotional one is not clear.

The Venerable Bede's (d.735) commentary on the unction of the sick is instructive. He links bodily sickness and faith-sickness as objects of healing. He writes that the bishop must bless the oil. While acknowledging that the laity can anoint themselves or others with consecrated oil, Bede argues that only the presbyters (priests) should administer this anointing because of the presence of sin that causes illness. It appears Bede wants to strengthen the role of presbyters and lessen anointing by the people, even when it would have been complicated getting priests to visit.[1]

Bede's connection between sin, sickness, anointing, and priesthood is significant. He uses 1 Corinthians 11:30 to show that people are made physically sick because of sin. If a person is sick because they are in sin, they need to confess to regain physical health. Such sin cannot be forgiven without confession, hence the argument for the priest. Consequently, Bede appears to connect the remission of sin in James's letter with penance rather than unction. But the necessity of confessing post-baptismal sins for Bede and our concept of daily sin may not be historically aligned.

Bede's approach is less confusing when one remembers that the anointing in James's letter was regarded and administered to complement the sacrament of penance. Bede's thinking reflects the widespread practice of canonical penance, tariff confession and penances. In Bede's context, confession was more critical than anointing because tariff confessions and penances were becoming more widely used. Thus, Bede's distinction between daily sins, which could be forgiven within the group of believers with daily prayer, and those sins that required the absolution of a priest, is instructive. Amalarius of Metz,[2] writing a century later and commenting on Bede's work, attributes the healing of sickness due to the unworthy reception of the Eucharist and the remission of daily sins to the power of the unction's prayer of faith.

Before the Carolingian liturgical reform, all Christians were permitted to anoint themselves and others in an emergency: *in sua aut in suorum necessitate*. By the mid-ninth century, anointing by the laity was forbidden, and priests were required to anoint the sick and dying. Because this was difficult in practice, the sacrament all but died out in many places. Once the obligation to administer it passed to the clergy, it became *extrema unctio* for the dying. By the time of Trent, critical voices from Orthodoxy and the reformers had been raised against extreme unction. Trent defended the sacramental truth of anointing against the reformers as the completion of a life of faithfulness and penance with special protection for the recipient. Chapter three of the *Doctrina de sacrament extremae unctionis* states that bishops and priests are the *ministri proprii* (own/proper/particular officials). This formulation does not exclude *ministri extraordinarii* (extraordinary officials).

The use of extraordinary ministers for the sacrament of the sick was raised before Vatican II by Archbishop Antonio Frondosa's (Capiz, the Philippines) decision to permit deacons to administer it. In the 1970s, the German Catholic Bishops' Conference requested two research documents on diaconal ministry and the anointing of the sick because they were worried about the growing shortage of priests and feared the sacrament would be forgotten. The research clarified two salient points: 1) that the reference in James 5:14 is not to priests; and 2) that Trent did not see the priest as the *only* minister but as the *proprius minister* (real, actual, appropriate minister), which did not exclude a *minister extraordinarius.*[3]

Although the laying on of the hand can be given without touching, the anointing is an essential, physical element of the rite. While in Covid situations it would be possible to anoint wearing gloves and protective clothing, the more critical question is whether lay ministers—primarily lay hospital chaplains—could be permitted to celebrate this sacrament in ordinary times. There is always a risk in applying an exceptional solution to an "ordinary" problem. However, physical mediation is needed for this sacrament.

These examples illustrate how the Covid experience challenges and changes our practice and thinking of sacramental mediation. The future may hold solutions for sacramental mediation taken from the earlier centuries of the Church. Because priests are "ordinarily" impeded from pastoral ministry, and parish communities are "ordinarily" unable to gather for Mass and other sacraments, our "ordinary" mediation of sacraments—our sacramental life—has already ground to a halt in many places. Given our extraordinary situation, we have a chance to think again.

Eucharist at Home

What would change in the Church if we considered ritual celebrations led by the laity in their own homes and with their neighbours? What would happen to the priesthood if a layperson led others in blessing the bread and wine, proclaiming the Gospel, blessing oil, giving absolution, and leading a Christian community in rites spoken on behalf of the Church, in union with the bishop? Would this be a more authentic sacramental experience than virtual masses, telephone confessions and zoom anointings in a time of necessity?

On his website, prayingeucharistically.com[4] , Fr James Alison's offered 'an invitation to an experiment which began on Palm Sunday 2020, as COVID confinement made it impossible for many people to attend acts of worship'. Alison states: 'rather than film myself celebrating Mass for my friends, and sharing the video, which seemed, to me at least, bizarrely clerical and pointless; or simply preparing video or audio of a homily for the Sunday readings and posting that; I felt that it may be time to try something a little bolder'.[5]

Alison offers a eucharistic service or Mass that individual believers or groups of believers can celebrate in their homes. He argues that instead of saying an online Mass, he is putting his 'presbyteral order' at the service of others 'by offering a structure to enable a new way of praying eucharistically for any members of the priesthood (that's all of us baptized, remember) who want to try it out'. This baptismal eucharistic celebration is essentially the celebration of the Roman Rite, with the baptised consecrating the elements and receiving them. The actual texts provided by Alison are, by and large, the texts of the 2000 translation, with all their anomalies and no evidence of creativity. Alison explains:

> I will provide, each week, the basic – and I'll keep it simple – text necessary for you (whether that is you singular, at home alone, or you plural, together with partner or family) to pray through the different steps of the Eucharist, from initial Blessing, through the readings, up to and including the consecration (yes, you'll be doing that) and consumption of the gifts, and final thanksgiving. Along with suggestions for how

> to make appropriate use of time, and how to
> space these different moments, I will provide
> also a video reading of the Gospel for the
> day. And I will provide a video homily of no
> more than 10 minutes.[6]

Alison's structure has three principles: first, there is 'no "laity" in Christianity' because all the baptised are conformed to 'Jesus the Great High Priest'; second, presbyters are here to serve and are not above the laity; and third the biblical principle of Emmaus hospitality, invitation and welcome of Christ into one's house and sharing with others. He offers 'a structure to enable a new way of praying eucharistically for any members of the priesthood (that's all of us baptized, remember) who want to try it out'. Alison argues that each baptised member has the 'ability to give thanks for what the Lord is giving us' each time we participate in the Eucharist. While this is true, it impedes the nature of the presences named in *Sacrosanctum Concilium* 7.

Alison's structure questions the priesthood as it is currently structured. Still, it clearly identifies the problem of a mediated sacramental system when those charged with mediation cannot be present. Alison argues that his objective is to give a new structure, cognisant of the unique times, to believers to pray eucharistically as "priests-in-baptism" during a time of crisis. He locates this in the theology of the priesthood of all believers and the character of baptism.

Alison supports his structure with the biblical motif of Emmaus and states you 'will host and be hosted by the risen Christ in your own home'. He acknowledges that his proposal,

> may sound so shocking, or at least surprising,
> to some Catholics, that they can pray the

words of institution, which they have been led to understand can only properly be pronounced by an ordained male, that I want to reassure you: Our Lord's instruction "Do this in memory of me" is not restrictive to a time, a place, a gender, or an ethnicity, but universal.

In confronting the absence of a valid and legal mediator in time of crisis, he is identifying the strength and the weakness of our mediated sacramental system. Our mediated sacramental system relies on an individual member's baptism, their ability to give praise and thanks, and it also relies on the ministry of liturgical leadership within the community. Sacraments are always mediated to us by another person in the name of the Church.

The weakness of Alison's approach is the conflation of baptism, eucharist, and priesthood. He suggests that because there "is no laity", we are all—through baptism—priests, making us all liturgical mediators or community presiders. There is more to the priesthood and liturgical ministry than just the fact of baptism, and his approach appears to undervalue this. In making his own priesthood available to others through this suggestion, Alison is still sharing a type of ministerial priesthood that, given the circumstances of Covid-19, cannot be shared. Baptism is, clearly, the sacrament of entry into the Church and the Eucharist, the sacrament of participation in the church. Both sacraments rely on the mediation of the Church—through the ministry of the ordained presider and the presence of the baptised church—so can we reduce the sacrament Eucharist to baptism?

Presiding at the Eucharist is not a private action but an ecclesial one given to the bishop and presbyter. Although baptism gives the character of leadership, it does not give the character of ordination. Alison addresses the question of obedience to the function of the priest/bishop as the confector of the sacrament of Eucharist, without whom it cannot be celebrated. Approaching this way, he reframes the question of presiding at the Eucharistic as one of discipline and ignores its ontological necessity as an element of liturgical presence. Thus, by amending one's understanding of the discipline of who has permission to preside and to speak the words of Institution and epiclesis, Alison moves the focus of the question. In doing so, he offers people the opportunity to take the permission to preside and confect the eucharist to themselves as baptised people:

> Historically we have structured obedience to it [the Institution Narrative] in varied ways over time, so it scarcely seems surprising that we have to re-structure our obedience at a time like this. What I am proposing and offering, for anyone who wants to take part, is simply an experimental re-structuring of our obedience in the present circumstances.

Alison says this is not 'in opposition to Mass, or even instead of Mass'. Rather, by 'stretching our obedience', we can remain connected to the Eucharist and not lose it from our lives. Loosed from the mooring of ordained ministry as the basis of liturgical presiding, we will 'have learned to take more responsibility for praying eucharistically, rather than delegating that responsibility to a shrinking clerical caste'. Here is the larger agenda; reforming the priesthood to serve in the contemporary church with an inclusive priesthood becomes apparent.

Two options of shared meals that are not considered the Eucharist—and not used by Alison, though probably form his background thinking—are the early church's custom of αγαπη, the agape meals, and the Orthodox custom of αντίδωρον having the faithful take home blessed bread. These are examples of ritualized customs related to the Eucharist but not, in fact, the Eucharist, for times like this when the eucharist is not available.

The agape feast or love feast is a communal meal shared by a Christian community. Its origins in the custom of the early church were an expression of fellowship. Evidence suggests it was initially part of the early Christian Eucharist. It was separated from the Eucharistic liturgy between the later first century and the mid-second century. It was intended to build unity and forgive past offences, but it was not without controversy.[7]

This communal, non-eucharistic meal has been used more recently in the Anglican and Methodist Churches. The *antidoron*, the leavened bread that is blessed but not consecrated and distributed at the end of the liturgy in churches that use the Byzantine Rite. *Antidoron* means "instead of gifts", that is, instead of the Eucharistic gifts. Because it is not consecrated during the Sacred Liturgy, it is not considered a sacrament; non-Orthodox attendees may share it as an expression of Christian fellowship and love.

Because Alison's offering uses already published texts, it may confuse people's understandings of the relationship between ordained priesthood and liturgical presiding. While his proposal questions the basis of the priesthood, it also offers a new view of it. Although his view does not take enough account of the relationship between liturgical-presiding and sacramental mediation, the larger question remains: is Alison offering a more authentic liturgical experience? Is he offering a sacred physical space by enabling people to use their own physical place as sacred? How one views his proposal depends entirely on one's understanding of the church, the sacraments, and the liturgy. Are they transactional or transformative experiences? Are they institutional acts or sacramental encounters?

---

1 Bede, Commentary on the Epistle of St. James, (P.L., XCIII, 39).

2 Amalarius of Metz, De Eccles. Offic., I, xii, in P.L., CV, 1011 sq.

3 Proprius, proprietary (English). Origin French propriétaire, from the Latin proprietarius, also proper; propre, Old French from the Latin proprius. Appropriate; to make one's own, from ad ("to") + proprio ("to make one's own").

4 Praying Eucharistically,
http://prayingeucharistically.com/ downloaded May 2021.

5 Praying Eucharistically.

6 Praying Eucharistically.

7 References to agape include 1 Corinthians, 11:17-34, Ignatius of Antioch's Letter to the Smyrnaeans and Pliny the Younger's letter to Trajan (ca 111 AD) where he writes: "on a stated day" in the early morning Christians "address a form of prayer to Christ, as to a divinity", and in "reassemble, to eat in common a harmless meal" which is taken to be the Agape. Similar communal meals are in the Apostolic tradition, though the term agape is not used and in the writing of Tertullian, where it is.

PART SIX
COMPETING
LITURGICAL MODELS

Models of Liturgy

Because liturgy is rich and complex, models help us discuss various approaches to it. In the 1970s and 1980s, James Empereur and Piet Fransen developed models of liturgy similar to Avery Dulles' church models.[1] Empereur outlines five models of liturgy as Institution, Mystery, Sacrament, Proclamation, and Process. All models have their limitations but also their points of clarity.

Although Empereur and Fransen offer five models (see Table Three below), I shall only focus on two of them—Liturgy as Institutional and Liturgy as Sacramental. I think these two are most represented in the liturgical response of Covid lockdown.

The models developed by Empereur and Fransen do not cover every aspect of liturgy because liturgy is a complex, rich, and multifaceted reality.

The models expose the operative ecclesiology or theology of the Church beneath the presumptions of how liturgy works. The models show who liturgy is constructed for and its role in the ecclesial power structure. Eventually, one model becomes dominant, defining sacraments, salvation, damnation, authority, and truth.

**Table Three. Models of Liturgy
(Empereur and Fransen)**

Model	Positive Aspect	Negative aspect
Institution	Necessity of structure	Rubricism
Mystery	Liturgical realism	Platonic separation of transcendent
Sacrament	Liturgy as social system communitarian	Sacramentalism God's work is broader than liturgy
Proclamation	Event of the Word of God	Biblical fundamentalism
Process	Liturgy as unity with life	Horizontalism and loss of relation to God.

Liturgical rites are used by believers to articulate their central theological concepts. We use liturgical rites to distinguish between orthodox and heterodox theologies and to authenticate or validate specific ministries and those who can exercise them. Rites are used to include and exclude.

The models help us clarify complex theological understandings that are not always immediately obvious. Exclusively preferencing one model over another is a mistake, writes Fransen, when he argues for a plurality of models:

> Models are symbols taken from our human experience....They help us either to discover aspects we have so far neglected or ignored or to structure and so to interpret a rather

complex reality. Since we definitely look at the Sacraments as symbolic activities, and not as 'signs' or symbols, taken from objects or things, the models we are going to use lend their expressive, inventive or interpretative function from the paradigmatic quality of some experienced human experience....Belonging further to the order of symbolic activity, models illuminate and explain the hidden or complex reality as much, maybe, as they obscure it. Therefore there is mostly a need for different models which complement and even correct one another.[2]

I have used Empereur and Fransen's models of liturgy as Institution and Sacrament. I have added my commentaries of liturgy as Transaction, Repeatable, and Ecclesial to them. But my comments are not fully rendered models like those of Empereur and Fransen. The model of liturgy as an institution has been the most prominent model throughout the liturgical lockdown for the following reasons.

Liturgy as Institution

The institutional model of liturgy's foundational ecclesiology sees the Church as a visible structure and offices identified with leadership and decision-making. It emphasises teaching, sanctifying, and governance. In this ecclesiology, liturgy is the preserve of the clergy, which they do *for* the people. Clergy are the source of grace that flows to the people who have a passive relationship to Grace and liturgy. Liturgy tends to become rigid and legalistic, and sanctification has legal dimensions one must observe. Liturgy is triumphalist, and there is little need for change.

The church is a perfect society, and theology's job is to defend the already correct belief. Liturgy's role is to celebrate this without any deviations.

In this model, grace is a performative attribute of sacramental ritual and priestly function. The reception of Grace relies on a mechanistic view. Grace is the product of the sacramental rites. It is like the toothpaste that comes out of its tube. The right toothpaste, on the right brush, in the correct mouth, with the right intention to let the toothpaste do its thing is essentially the model. The sacraments are the means for attaining Grace, which is produced *ex opere operato*.

Before the fifth century, the word *sacramentum* was not a uniquely Christian term and embraced every mystical and sacred thing *omne mysticum sacrumque signum*. After the fifth century, *sacramentum* was applied primarily to forms of worship instituted by Christ through which divine blessings are mystically represented, sealed, and given to an individual. St Augustine was the first to offer a more precise theology of the nature of the sacraments and defined a sacrament as the visible sign of an invisible grace or divine blessing.

According to Augustine, sacraments have two constitutive elements: first, a sensible element— known to or by the senses is called the *signum*,[3] experienced by the person and seen by others; and second, the inward grace or virtue (the *res* or *virtus sacramenti*), an object of faith, and these are united by the word of consecration.[4]

Augustine also framed a distinct doctrine of how the sacraments operate. In his view, the sacraments give grace or condemnation, blessing or curse, according to the receiver's condition or intention. Sacraments do not act immediately and magically, but mediately and ethically, not *ex opere operato*, in the later scholastic language, but through the medium of the active faith of the receiver. Sacraments have their objective reality. They do not depend on the subjective condition of the one who administers them because they are divine institutions that give blessing to those who ask for them in faith. Thus, for Augustine, faith is the subjective condition of receiving Grace.

Although Augustine's distinction between a transient and a permanent effect of the sacrament prepared the way for the scholastic's doctrine of indelible character, the popular opinion was already intensely superstitious. It saw sacraments as magical operations of God. According to St Augustine's maxim, sacraments are primarily understood as *signum visibilia invisibilies gratiae* (visible signs of the invisible grace). Augustine applied his understanding of scripture, where the ritual action and the ritual words make a single element to his notion of sacraments.

Later, theologians took up Augustine's work and built on it. Later scholastics framed the notion of sacraments using terms from Aristotelian philosophy such as *esse* and *essence* and matter and form. In later centuries the unity of material elements (*materia*) and words (*forma*) was critical to producing a sacramental action and its effect called Grace. A legalistic mindset developed. It saw the relationship of matter and spirit (phenomena or *elementum* and the words, or *verbum*), joined with intentionality and legally performed by the priest, essential to the giving or performance of a sacrament (*accedit verbum ad elementum et fit sacramentum*).

The later scholastic model went through variations. In its neo-scholastic form, it has created—and maintained—a liturgical model that relies on an essential distinction between what is *done* by the clergy and what is *received* by the people. Liturgy is a pyramidal event with the ranks of the clergy dispensing grace through their traditional ritual functions. Worshippers are given a passive position of sitting, listening, and receiving from the clergy, their source of liturgical benefaction. The division between the clergy and the laity is illustrated architecturally in the church building's shape, topography, and architectural divisions, such as the processional ways and the sanctuary and its steps.

The sanctifying power of the sacraments is dependent on the proper observance of the law and the proper administration of the sacrament, which can only be "done" by the officially designated person. This model of Church drives a model of the priesthood as well. Liturgy tends to become legalistic, and the priest, too, is bound by laws that ensure that he does not impose himself into the celebration of the rites. The priest's active role at the centre of the liturgy and the peoples' passive participation in the liturgy is illustrated by the reception of holy communion. While the priest can separate the reception of holy communion for the laity from praying the Eucharistic Prayer, as in drive-up communion, he will not do this for himself. While the priest is 'bound' to receive the elements consecrated on the altar during the Mass at the Communion Rite, it is 'most desirable that the faithful' do the same, but not absolute. Many priests who give the pre-consecrated sacrament as holy communion to the laity at Mass will not receive it themselves. To do so would break the validity of their Mass. Here, the priority of the priest over the laity and the inability to bring the theology of the liturgy to life in the praxis of the liturgy come together. This type of thinking allowed the concept of drive-up communion and spiritual communion to blossom during the lockdown.

This legalistic view of liturgy is alive and strong because it gives stability in a rapidly changing world. Although there is little scriptural evidence to support this model of Church, and although it struggles in a pluralistic society, it has been operative in many of our liturgical responses throughout Covid lockdown. It reinforces clericalism in liturgy and does not fret the absence of the laity. Fidelity to the rubrics is paramount for the sacrament's validity, which is more important than the quality of the celebration itself. The expression of this model is the *missa privata,* with the priest responding to himself. There is very little room for practical ecumenism in this model because other churches are approached with a fundamental suspicion that their institution is not equal in theology. Their worship is not equal in Grace to that of the authentic institution.

The institutional model tends to freeze liturgy in ritual books. And it reinforces a clericalist approach to liturgy and sacraments. This is not unusual, as all institutions tend toward calcification and legal purification of their rituals to control their use. Legitimate, lawful, or permitted performance of rites is given to delegated individuals who then further manage those who can and cannot function ritually. The hallmark of orthodoxy for many is correct thinking leading to correct acting and expressed in rubrical precision and worship. This approach does not consider the nature of orthodoxy as right or correct praise. Where this is true, faithfulness to the letter of the rubric is more desirable than the efficacy of the prayer. This tendency reduces both the laity and the clergy to sums of their functions in the liturgical and church world. In this view, liturgy has little need to change, and anthropological models of prayer are generally ignored. This view of the liturgy is observable in many church documents, including those of the Second Vatican Council. However, this tendency is moderated by the Council's pastoral theology and its communion-ecclesiology.

Liturgy as Sacrament

The sacramental model of the liturgy is one of the most widely practised. It is the operative model in the liturgical theology of the Second Vatican Council that has been used and modified since. In this model, the Church is the primordial sacrament. The liturgy that stands at the heart of the Church's life is understood in a narrow sense as sacramental. Because the nature of the Church as a sacrament is expressed through her relationship to Christ, sacramentality, sacraments, and liturgy all share an anthropological or human dynamic.

The Dogmatic Constitution on the Church, Lumen Gentium, article one describes it:

> Since the church, in Christ, is a sacrament— a sign and instrument, that is, of communion with God and of the unity of the entire human race—it here proposed, for the benefit of the faithful and of the entire world, to describe more clearly, and in the tradition laid down by earlier council, its own nature and universal mission. The present situation lends greater urgency to this duty of the church, so that all people, who nowadays are drawn ever more closely together by social, technical and cultural bonds, may achieve full unity in Christ.[5]

Sacrosanctum Concilium, 10, articulates the interrelationship of liturgy and Church to those who worship and thus to the world:

> the liturgy is the summit towards the activity of the church is directed; it is also the source from which all its power flows. For the goal of apostolic endeavor is that all who are made children of God by faith and baptism should come together to praise God in the midst of this church....The liturgy, in its turn, moves the faithful filled with "the paschal sacraments" to be "one in their commitment to you (God)"....From the liturgy...and especially from the Eucharist, grace is poured forth upon us as from a fountain, and our sanctification in Christ and the glorification of God to which all other activities of the church are directed, as toward their end, are achieved with maximum effectiveness.[6]

The sacramental model understands that all human life is symbolic, and each individual manifests the divine. We encounter the mysterion of God in relationship to the mysterion of the individual. Thus, we encounter each individual person as a theological reality where God is present and comes more fully into view the more the individual seeks to live in the presence of God. This antho-divine relationship is based on the theology of the incarnation giving us an antho-divine mysterion. This is the bedrock of the sacramentality of the liturgy and this model. Consequently, like Christ, the individual person and the liturgy become signs and symbols of communion with God.

The antho-divine mysterion is at work in creation. It is made explicit or visible in the sacramental-liturgical rites, which are bodily, corporeal expressions for the individual within the community that mediates them. The human person is the meeting point of the material and the divine because the human person is the antho-divine mysterion. For the experience of sacramental-liturgical mediation to be effective, a prior experience of personal conversion is necessary within the individual; a turning towards God and being turned towards God. The double dynamic of turning—oneself—and of being turned—by God—illustrates that sacraments are more than rites by which or through which Grace is transferred. Sacraments are names we give to the awakening of the antho-divine mysterion.

In the liturgical act, the presence of God is made manifest through the use of rites and rituals. The awakening of the antho-divine mysterion is then given ritual forms that express this and make it manifest through bodily actions. In the model of liturgy as a sacrament, the liturgy is more than a sum of its parts because it is an expression of leitourgia that points to something greater. It becomes the efficacious sign that intensifies what it brings to expression.

The sacramental model of the liturgy is dialogical. Sacraments and their attendant rites are social symbols as well as religious ones. They are social and dialogical because God is seen as a participant in social, human interaction. The sacraments "give" God "a human face" because they live in an individual believer and in the community of believers. The sacrament at its organic level is an "encounter" between an individual and God.

This is a moment of conversion when an individual turns themself towards God, and God turns the individual towards the divinity. An organic or primal encounter underpins the formal or liturgical celebration. Encounter names the sacramentality of the experience. Next comes the formal or liturgical encounter of the sacramental rite when the primal or organic is given liturgical form through ritual.

The prior conversion—turning towards God and being turned by God—takes on an external, ritualised form in the liturgy when it articulates the prior conversion in the company of the Body of Christ. The liturgical ritualisation brings together in a unity of shared experience the individual conversion, the community's faith, and God's presence.

At the visible level, liturgical rites are an encounter between God, an individual and the community of faith. Consequently, they are not private, individual experiences or possessions. They are communal symbols of encounter that bring the life of Grace to visibility. Because sacraments are communal, they are mediated by the community and its minister to the recipient. Thus, we do not anoint or baptise ourselves, and everyone, apart from the presiding minister, receives communion and does not take it. When we look at sacraments, and the sacramentality of liturgy from this perspective, is it clear why the celebration of the Eucharist, alone, by a single priest is an incomplete sign.

This model uses the metaphors of the Body of Christ and the People of God extensively to explain and explore liturgy as the corporate act of a community. These metaphors clarify why the baptised assembly is both the recipient and minister of the sacrament and emphasise sacramental encounter as a spirit-filled fellowship in Christ. A liturgical theology based on this understanding emphasises the union of Grace—conversion—at the personal level that is made visible at the corporate level through the ministry of the community. In this model, liturgy is not juridically focused, neither is the institution of the

Church the primary focus. The liturgy, as the act of the believer, the believers, and God. It is a spirit-based encounter of persons in the society of the created order.

When taken to an extreme, the chief weakness of this model reduces the liturgical encounter to a human or anthropological gesture that invites God to participate. This weakness is seen in the false pastoral solution that ignores the need for primal conversion. When baptism is used as a "pastoral solution", the recipient and the community remain distanced. When baptism is given as the initiator of conversion and is not its signifier, the hard work of conversion has not been done. When the liturgical rites are not anchored in conversion, they become anthropological or humanistic expressions of an individual or their family's understanding of the sacrament.

Where the community is understood to be more than a social or human phenomenon, the sacramentality of liturgy enables the liturgy—through her rites—to express the profound, eschatological union between God and humankind at the heart of the Incarnation. The liturgy celebrates Grace as a communal gift. For the liturgy to be sacramental, it must be anchored to its own sacramentality and express the characteristics of leitourgia.

The sacramental liturgy makes visible communal and incarnated signs accessible to the senses and understandable to those receiving them when it celebrates an authentic synergy between the individual's conversion, the community's faith and ministry, and the mediation of Grace anchored in the Trinity. Liturgical rites are structured to show this relationship and call it purposefully to mind. The rituals must be structured to enable people to participate in them and know them as realisations of Grace. In the liturgical act, something must happen—expression and awareness come together—in the lives of the worshippers.

This approach does not claim a monopoly on Grace for the liturgy because Grace, which in Greek is called *charis,* is an undeserved and graciously given gift. The love that reciprocates from the human side is called *Caritas*, which results from the divine blessing. This gift of the Trinity, Father, Son, and Spirit means that the Father, Son, and Spirit live within us as the source and origin of our participation in the divine life. Thus, Grace and salvation are found beyond the Church and the liturgy. But this model still affirms that the liturgy is the most explicit articulation of the Christian experience of God because it is the prayer of Christ. Christ and the Church as sacraments of God's reconciliation are a statement that God's reconciling love, seen in the Paschal Mystery and the Event of the Cross, is an epiphany of the presence of God. Grace always seeks to be visible, and liturgical rites give visibility. Other visible signs of Grace are feeding the hungry and bringing peace to violence because these are also manifestations of salvation.

Other manifestations of salvation are essential to ensure that liturgy does not become a specialist event of a perfect society. References to liturgy as a heavenly dimension on earth can tend to take the sacramental model beyond the reach of most people. Liturgy also has an ethical dimension, as do the sacraments. One has to be careful not to idealise the communal aspect of liturgy to the point that it cannot deal with its imperfection. Liturgy is not dressage; it is the sometimes-bumpy expression of ordinary people at prayer. Liturgy does not require an already perfected community to celebrate. Instead, it requires a community open to perfection through their participation in the mystery of God, at the centre of their worship.

The sacraments, expressed liturgically, are not private events or personal ways to salvation or heaven. By their nature, they are ecclesial events and have an ecclesial function. They sanctify us by bringing us together, which is central to the celebration of the Eucharist. The reason for private worship is based implicitly on the idea of private Grace and personal sanctification. It leads some people to seek out, even in the Mass, a "me and Jesus moment" where the world can legitimately be left behind or ignored and where the community is an intrusion.

In the sacramental model, salvation is a communal reality. It distinguishes itself from the institutional model's individualistic view of salvation because God has created us within the human family, and it is within that family that we are saved. The symbolic nature of human existence is incarnational. Experiences of living and salvation are intimately intertwined in the fabric of life. There is an intrinsic relationship between the mystery of God and the mystery of human existence, between theology and anthropology.

The liturgical act—as the sacramental expression of salvation—is where men and women are saved (SC2). The liturgy is the intersection and convergence of salvation, Grace, ritual, response, praise, and charity. It is precisely in the experience of the liturgy as the sacramental rite and in the liturgy's sacramentality that we encounter the theologies of Trinity, Incarnation, Christology, Pneumatology, and Eschatology as doorways to God. We encounter them in the liturgy as articulations of the mysterion we worship. We are immersed in the mysterion because liturgy *articulates them all.* But it is the liturgy as ecclesiology that connects Trinty, Incarnation, Christology, Pneumatology (theology of the Holy Spirit), and Eschatology (theology of the final things) with soteriology (the doctrine of salvation) and the teaching of the ongoing presence of Christ, in and with the Church, for each believer.

Because the liturgy is an act of the entire baptised community, it is the relational place between God and humankind. It is an ecclesial place—a place of the Church, where understandings of Church collide. Liturgy is ecclesiology; it is never neutral because the people who attend to it are believers who are never neutral! Liturgy does not express faith as an intellectual concept but as a lived experience because it brings to mind, recalls, and presents the lived experience of being human with others, in God. This is the sacramentality of the liturgy. At this deep level, the Sacred Liturgy, the liturgies of the sacraments and all forms of the Church's public prayer are participative experiences that embody the dialogue between the divine and the human. They are places where we encounter the priesthood and the liturgical presence of Christ in what we call the Paschal Mystery.[7]

The Paschal Mystery is revealed in several ways: first, it is prefigured in the Hebrew scriptures; second, it is given the historical presence in the life of Jesus of Nazareth recorded in the Christian scriptures; thirdly, it is contained in the liturgical-sacramental rites and lived in the faith of the Body of Christ and made known in the mission and work of the Church. Finally, it is fulfilled in the eschatological promise where Christ is "all in all" and all things are laid at the Father's feet. Christians access this mysterion in multiple ways:

through the scriptures and the liturgy, through their lives of and good works and prayer and mysticism.

The Christian sacraments are the most profound form of revelation of Grace. They are an epiphany of Grace and salvation. The redemptive Paschal Mystery is offered to the person of faith and the community of faith. Grace's presence in the created order is revealed in the mysterion of Christ. He is the perfect response of humankind to the Father made manifest in the liturgical-sacramental rites. Christ is the epiphany of redemption, and in the liturgy, his redeeming life, death, and resurrection are expressed sacramentally. In this way, liturgy is prophetic.

In the thinking of Karl Rahner, Grace becomes visible in the history of people of faith, even where that faith is lived "anonymously". He writes of the world as the place where men and women, endowed with spiritual capacity, freely accept or decline God's revelation. In our world, redeemed and reconciled to God, the sacraments do not operate from outside the world, like a light penetrating the darkness; instead, they are the light within the world, illuminating God's presence. Because the sacraments operate from within this reconciled world, Grace is not an extraordinary intervention that penetrates from the outside; Grace is the yeast in the bread of everyday life. The liturgical-sacramental actualisation shows Grace to be relational, dynamic, and participatory.

Liturgy as Function

Functionalistic liturgy is a type that relies on the ritual as its primary transmitter. While ritual transmits the function of prayer, ceremony alone does not create sacramental efficacy. While rituals express conversion (*metanoia*), communion (*koinonia*), and salvation (*soteria*), they are not the sources of these.[8] Functional worship tends to look at rituals as the means of getting something done or getting grace transacted between the parties. The functionalist approach to the sacraments has three main characteristics: first, it views sacraments as a "thing to be done" primarily in a one-way communication pattern; second, it sees sacramental celebration as secondary to the function of cult as the direct action of the priest who is the intermediary; third, it is utterly pragmatic where "pastoral reasons" can justify the jettisoning of sound scriptural, theological, and historical sources when required.

For example, a functionalist approach to baptism is more interested in salvation from sin, limbo, or hell than in a vocational call to participate in God's work of redemption. Private baptisms do not want to place themselves liturgically in the Sunday assembly because the function of the family is the reason for the baptism. Similarly, special group masses have the role of the group at heart, and the Mass is entertainment. This approach reduces the Eucharist to "saying Mass", emphasising the overriding presumption of *getting something done for a good cause—for the life of the particular group*. The cleric who sees the Mass as his preserve or act of piety uses it functionally as part of his private prayer structure, often at a time that suits him. Although Covid-19 allowed the functionalist approach to liturgy and sacraments to grow during the lockdown, it did not create it. The roots of functionalism lie deep within the psyche of the Church.

Liturgy as Transaction

The transactional form of worship is observable in the ways people talk about liturgy in ordinary discourse. When people speak of liturgy, they generally talk about ritual actions, such as putting the chalice on the altar or whether the cantor should sing the psalm at the ambo. These questions are incidentally liturgical and essentially ritualistic because liturgy is a much more extensive engagement with the work of God for which worship is the response.

In most parishes, the Mass is a function of parish life. Even when the priest is not available to preside, functionality demands what for many is the alternative form of Mass, the Liturgy of Word with holy communion. Within parishes, functionalism promotes a "me and Jesus" piety that brings with it the demand for additional or special masses and the inclusion of private devotions in public worship. The sacramental rite of Reconciliation and Penance is one of the more functional forms of liturgy that has an intensely transactional nature for many people. It is still the place to bargain with God in the sense that both sin and forgiveness are transactional: "if I do this, will I still get to heaven?" Where this is present, the demand to leave aside the scriptures and not celebrate them with the Liturgy of the Word is strong.

Transactional thinking enabled the easy transference of the Mass to the virtual environment because it sees the Mass as an essential element of the parish or clerical life. The Mass's ritual programme—a series of ritual actions in a programmatic pattern of predictable words, gestures, and movement—gives it a standard, repetitive form. More than this, the transactional thinking comfortably reduces the role of liturgical presider to the priest at the altar and the four liturgical foci of the ambo, altar, chair, and assembly to the priest at his dining table or altar.

Like functionalism, transactional thinking promotes a passive form of prayer, where the congregation is the observer. The vulnerability of the Eucharist is its uniqueness as an oft-received sacrament. This is its gift, but it also makes it vulnerable to liturgical individualism and functionalism. Frequency and accessibility have led to overuse. They have bred a subtle form of individualistic liturgical functionalism.

Liturgy as Repeatable

The proliferation of virtual masses exposed a functionalist and transactional agenda in worship; this is the operative theology of liturgy. The frequency of the Mass, related to its repeatability and accessibility, makes it vulnerable to overuse. It is not wrong to celebrate Mass, but is it worth considering whether we are using the Mass as a tool of church living rather than the summit and source of church life? It is worth considering why during the Covid lockdown, we could not set aside the celebration of the Mass and turned to substitutional forms. The following brief historical outline may help.

Many historical sources have formed the eucharistic practice of the Eastern and Western Churches. Before the Middle Ages, various practices and reasons influenced daily and Sunday masses in the Western Church. For some, the necessity to provide enough masses for the local population on Sundays, saints days, and civil festivals drove the multiplication of masses. For others, the desire to celebrate Mass with smaller groups outside the parish, as at the graves of the dead, or celebrate votive masses, led to various masses observed and increased frequency.

The roots of our current practice can be found in the reaction to the Reformation and post-reformation European religious wars. The need to defend Catholic eucharistic theology resulted in a fortress mentality building within Catholic circles that concretised theological thinking and liturgical practice. The increasing emphasis on the fruit of the Mass for the priest and through him for the laity changed the approach to the Mass. Mass became less of a parish event and more the solution to all spiritual problems. It became a cultic event to be celebrated any day, at any time, in any place, for any reason, by any priest, for himself or others, with or without an attending congregation. It became a product of priesthood and holiness and the Church. Instead of being the outcome of prayer and belief, it became the product that typified these. Mass became a function of religion rather than its expression.

Over time, the notion of multiple masses in the same church for numerous reasons without communion for laity took hold. It was a significant move away from the earlier practice of a single, daily Mass with communion for all attending. Evidence shows how eucharistic piety and practice changed with the eventual effect that the laity's full participation and reception of communion were lost. In large urban areas and major churches, the side-altars masses became the venues of multiple masses, some sung, some spoken, and others silent, often with people moving between them. As the ordinary function of the Mass moved to become the celebration by the priest for the people, the number of masses increased, reflecting the growing theology of fear of eternal damnation. Masses were offered for the salvation of souls, reparation for the dead, and preservation from Hell's fire and often without the donor being present. As the practice of massing priests grew, so did the permission for priests to celebrate several masses each day.

By the late 19th century and into the 20th, the legal—but not binding requirement—for priests to celebrate daily Mass as part of their personal prayer increased the number of masses. The pious Catholic laity was also encouraged to avail themselves of the daily Mass. Daily Mass was already a standard element of parish life by the Second Vatican Council, and Catholic identity was deeply related to the Mass. Following the Council, the proliferation of generational and evangelising masses became the norm with mass for the women's or men's group, home masses, charismatic masses, special masses, and school masses. Mass was used to evangelise, catechize, and promote many things. Now we are subjected to Mission Sunday, Life Sunday, Word Sunday, Vocations Sunday, Marriage Sunday, the list goes on... Each particular cause identified that the instigators do not really understand the nature of the Mass. This attempt to make the Mass accessible and relevant to all also had a negative impact by promoting the notion that Mass is the only form of prayer available to Catholics. At the same time, priests became freer of the "obligation" to celebrate Mass every day. So arose the priest's Monday off and the prayer service led by the laity.

Although the Second Vatican Council firmly directed a return to the community character of the Mass for both priest and laity by offering concelebration for the clergy and giving greater access to lay ministry and holy communion for the laity, it nonetheless supported the daily Mass of the priest. Its Decree on the Ministry and Life of Priests, *Presybterium Ordinis,* states that the first task of the priest is the 'apostolic proclamation of the Gospel' which is 'completed in union with the sacrifice of Christ...in the Eucharist...offered through the priests.'[9]

In Chapter Two, under the subtitle 'functions of the priests', the first function is as ministers of the Word of God:

> The people of God is formed into one in the first place by the word of the living God, which is quite rightly expected from the mouth of priests, of since nobody can be saved who has not first believed, it is the first task of priests as co-workers of the bishops to preach the Gospel of God to all.[10]

The priest's second function is explored in the context of the role's relationship to the Eucharist through sacramental ministry and the Eucharist, which also references the liturgy:

> The purpose then, for which priests are consecrated by God through the ministry of the bishop is that they should be made sharers in a special way in Christ's priesthood and, by carrying out sacred functions, act as ministers of him who through his Spirit continually exercises his priestly role for our benefit in the liturgy.[11]

Although the proclamation of the Gospel comes first, it is directed to the Eucharist:

> all ecclesiastical ministries and works of the apostolate are bound up with the Eucharist and directed to it. For in the most blessed Eucharist is contained the entire spiritual wealth of the church, namely Christ himself our Pasch and our living bread.[12]

Later in the Decree, the primary role of being ministers of the word of God is trumped, again, by the ministry of the Mass. One can read here the almost verbatim source of the Canon Law quoted earlier:

> In the mystery of the eucharistic sacrifice, in which priests fulfil their principal function, the work of our redemption is continually carried out. For this reason, the daily celebration of the Eucharist is earnestly recommended. This celebration is an action of Christ and the church, even if it is impossible for the faithful to be present. So, when priests unite themselves with the action of Christ the Priest, they daily offer themselves completely to God, and by being nourished with Christ's body, they share in the charity of him who gives himself as food to the faithful.[13]

The tension between the presbyter and the cultic priest is throughout the Decree. One sees the tension between the priest's role as minister of God's word and his role as a sacrificial priest. Although the Decree attempts to give the proclamation of the Word a new prominence, one gets the sense that it can only do this at the expense of eucharistic ministry. While the desire to make the 'apostolic proclamation of the Gospel' priesthood's primary function is present, the leadership of the eucharistic sacrifice is the primary function.

Presbyterorum Ordinis focuses on priestly ministry while holding to the traditional value. It struggles to articulate the relationship between the first and second functions of priesthood and the importance of one over the other. Because it doesn't achieve this, it reverts to the cultic function of the priesthood. This is not surprising, but it is also confusing. Consequently, it struggles to articulate a more refined understanding of the relationship between the 'celebration [of the liturgy as] an action of Christ and the church'. Leaving the presence of the 'faithful' aside when they cannot be present does not impede the priest from celebrating Mass even if 'the eucharistic celebration is the center of the assembly of the faithful over which the priest presides'.[14] In the end, this sums up the contemporary situation and underpins our current approach to the Mass.

Lurking underneath is the suspicion that priesthood needs the Mass as its reason for existence. The clergy need the Mass more than the laity. The theologies of priesthood and church presented here do not include the laity at the same level. Therein lies the ultimate problem we are encountering in the liturgical responses to Covid. The Mass is primarily for the priest and not for the laity. This thinking expects priests to celebrate daily Mass irrespective of the values inherent in community, gathering, sacramentality in public worship. Indeed, not celebrating a daily Mass can be more problematic for a priest and less understood than sounder theology. Mass is the identifiable task of priests; it is what they do, and doing it forms them. Consideration of the pastoral need for the Mass is an oft-forgotten criterion for celebrating the Mass. People forget that while the Mass is the source and summit of Christian worship, it is not the Church's only form of prayer. Ignoring this has led to a situation where other forms of worship, like the Divine Office, can barely find a place in the daily calendar, especially on Sundays.

Liturgy as Ecclesiology

The ecclesial dimension is decisive in understanding how liturgy works and its use. A person's ecclesial understanding of the Church is a powerful determiner of whether they tend towards an Institutional or Sacrament Model of liturgy and sacraments. A vision of the Church is important because it is an accessible classifier for people: what type of Church have you signed up to; what sort of Church do you want for yourself and your family; what kind of Church gives you the songs, music, homilies, and ceremonial you want; what sort of Church do you wish to identify with as a Christian and as a Catholic? These questions and our responses to them create an ecclesial identity.

Liturgy, prayer, and worship function ecclesially. Liturgical-sacramental rites are both inclusive and exclusory. For example, the baptised receive holy communion, but the non-baptised do not. The lex orandi—how and what we pray—is also determined by how one views the role of worship in the Church. Liturgy also distinguishes one ecclesial community from another. The Liturgy formally presented creates an orthodoxy that separates denominations within the Christian Church and ecclesial communities and liturgical styles within the Latin Church. One of the clearest examples of this was the distinction of "ordinary" and "extraordinary" rites, made by Benedict XVI in 2007 until it was abolished by Pope Francis in 2021.

Benedict's distinction created a competitive hierarchy between the 1962 and 1970 rites of the Mass. It consolidated an antagonistic, stylistic distinction between "progressive" and "traditionalist" Catholics, based on their preferred liturgical form and the divisive categories of "ordinary" and "extraordinary" took on a quasi-theological status. The distinction was intended to allow two different ritual forms of the lex orandi to exist simultaneously in the Latin Church under the falsehood that this allowed for organic development. The distinction was intended to show that the Church could understand herself ecclesiologically as faithful to the Second Vatican Council and rejecting it.

As a consequence, ecclesial disunity grew within the Church. Pope Francis' Motu Proprio *Traditionis Custodes* (*Guardians of the Tradition*)[15] limited the use of the 1962 Roman Missal and revoked the concessions and the distinctions of Benedict's *Summorum Pontificum*. *Traditionis Custodes* restates that the liturgical books issued by Popes Paul VI and John Paul II are 'the unique expression of the lex orandi [law of prayer] of the Roman Rite'.[16] In doing so, he nullifies the distinctions of ordinary and extraordinary forms.

He stipulated that the only pre-conciliar Mass form that may be used is the 1962 Roman Missal published by Pope John XXIII because some were going back to other suppressed forms of the Mass. He explains that his decision is to restore the unity of the church's ecclesial expression, 'the principal expression of the lex orandi of the Roman Rite [functions] to maintain the unity of the Church'.

By ensuring there is 'a single and identical prayer,' Pope Francis clarified the relationship between ecclesiology and liturgy that, sadly, *Summorum Pontificum* had blurred by sanctioning the pretence of two forms of the one rite coexisting in a single liturgical family. By not making the older rite a liturgical rite in its own right—akin to a rite of the Eastern Catholic Churches—*Summorum Pontificum* sort to avoid division. However, it still contributed to a competitive ecclesial world in the end. It deepened the liturgical division and contributed to a corrosive, ecclesial life.

The divisions were essentially ones of ecclesiology, not liturgy. The distinct ecclesiology underpinnings separating the 1962 and 1970

Roman Missals define adherents. Liturgical texts are potent ecclesial texts that articulate the nature of revelation—who is God and how is God present in Christ and the Church. These are the texts they pray and the formulations of the Church, God, and belief that they identify with sacramentally. The ecclesial distinctions between these two texts can be seen in their ritual structures. Specific texts, like Good Friday's intercessions: the 1962 Missal speaks of the perfidious Jews, 'Oremus et pro perfidis Iudaeis',[17] but the present translation of the 1970 Missal's Good Friday rites refers to them as those 'to whom the Lord our God spoke first'.[18] Where the pre-conciliar rites presume that only the priest is praying the Mass, saying all the readings and prayers either aloud or silently himself, the post-conciliar liturgy assumes that all attendees are praying the Mass, with the lectors, deacons, and lay readers proclaiming the readings and the priest praying the presidential prayers and eucharistic prayers aloud. These are not just ritual differences; they are ecclesial icons of meaning that define who worships, how they worship and for whom they worship.

Thus, every believer understands the liturgy at many intersecting points. Each intersection is a place where the believer knows him or herself as both believer and Catholic because the liturgy is an ecclesial act—an act of the Church. Liturgy is the multifaceted act of the entire community of the baptised. It gets further complicated by each person's unique understanding of salvation and redemption, the purpose of worship, and ultimately who God is and how God saves. An individual's understanding of liturgy's sacramentality determines how they approach it from an ecclesial understanding. Their knowledge of liturgy's symbolic and sign value—its corporate character—determines how they view the Church as a community, an institution, or the Mystical Body of Christ.

This panorama shapes how recipients of sacraments receive them as visible articulations of Grace in liturgical signs and symbols in an individual life. An individual's unique understanding of how liturgy works sacramentally—in sacramental-liturgical rites—as expressions of Grace and salvation is foundational to their concept of God. Liturgy brings us back to the participative experience of salvation when it articulates—ritually—the double movement of redemption of God's descent (*exitus*) in the sanctification of the world and the return (*reditus*) of the individual in worship for which Christ is the perfect exemplar. As God, Christ offers God's salvation to the world, and as a human being, in obedience, he gives thanks to the Father in a perfect response.

Liturgy celebrates this mysterion in the ecclesiastical sacraments that it mediates through sign and symbol. The sacraments are liturgical-ecclesial acts that make the glorified presence of Christ visible; through the liturgical rites, the sacraments give Grace and offer salvation to all people. The liturgical rites make sacramental grace known through signs and symbols. The recipients of these sacred rites give thanksgiving and praise to the Father, in Christ, and through the Holy Spirit. They are witnesses to the mysterion, through which they know themselves to be participants in the life and leitourgia of God.

1 James Empereur, "Models of a Liturgical Theology" in The Sacraments: Readings in Contemporary Sacramental Theology, New York, 1981, pp53-70; Piet Fransen, "Sacraments as Celebrations" in Irish Theological Quarterly 43 (1976) pp151-170; Avery Dulles, Models of the Church, Doubleday and Co, Garden City, 1974.

2 Piet Fransen, "Sacraments as Celebrations" in Irish Theological Quarterly 43, (1976), pp151-170, 151.

3 Also, sacramentum in the stricter sense.

4 Signum visibile, or forma visibilis gratiae invisibilis. Augustine calls the sacraments also verba visibilia, signacula corporalia, signa rerum spiritualium, signacula rerum divinarum visibilia. See, Augustine, De catechiz. rudibus, § 50: "Sacramenta signacula quidem rerum divinarum esse visibilia, sed res ipsas invisibiles in eis honoari." Serm. ad pop. 292 (tom. v. p. 770): "Dicuntur sacramenta, quia in eis aliud videtur, aliud intelligitur. Quod videtur, speciem habet corporalem; quod intelligitur, fructum habet spiritalem."
Augustine, In Joann Evang. tract. 80: "Detrahe verbum, et quid est aqua [the baptismal water] nisi aqua? Accedit verbum ad elementum et fit sacramemtum, etiam ipsum tamquam visibile verbum."

5 Dogmatic Constitution on the Church, Lumen Gentium 21 November 1964, in The Basic Sixteen Documents, Vatican II, Constitutions, Decrees, Declarations, A. Flannery, ed., (New York, Dublin: Costello Publishing and Dominican Publications,1996), Chapter I, 1.

6 SC., 10, 122.

7 SC., 7, 120. To accomplish so great a work, Christ is always present in his church, especially in its liturgical celebrations. He is present in the sacrifice of the Mass both in the person of his minister, "the same now offering through the ministry of priest, who formerly offered himself on the cross," and most of all in the eucharistic species, But his power he is present in the sacraments so that when anybody baptises it is really Christ himself who baptizes. He is present in his word

since it is he himself who speaks when the holy scripture are read in church. Lastly, he is present when the church prayer and sings, for he has promised "where two or three are gathered together in my name there am I in the midst of them" (Mat 18:20)

8 Metanoia means a changing of one's heart or mind and thus of one's way of living. Koinonia means Christian fellowship or a body of believers sharing their religious and spiritual life.

9 PO., 318.

10 PO., 323.

11 PO., 324.

12 PO., 325.

13 PO., 346.

14 PO., 325.

15 Pope Francis, Traditionis Custodes, Apostolic Letter Issues Motu Proprio, On the Use of the Roman Liturgy Prior to the Reform of 1970, 16 July, 2021.

16 To protect the unity of the Body of Christ Francis was 'constrained to revoke the faculty granted by my Predecessors…granting the freedom to celebrate the Mass with the Missale Romanum of 1962'. His decision to 'abrogate all the norms, instructions, permissions and customs that precede the present motu proprio, and declare that the liturgical books promulgated by the saintly Pontiffs Paul VI and John Paul II, in conformity with the decrees of Vatican Council II, constitute the unique expression of the lex orandi [law of prayer] of the Roman Rite' shows he clearly understands the ecclesial dimension of the lex orandi—as his predecessor Pope Paul did when he refused to allow the pre-conciliar rite. The relationship between liturgy as an ecclesial act and the liturgy as the symbol of my conception of the Church is intimate.

17 Prayer 8, Pro conversion Iudaeorum, Missale Romanum XVI, Editio Taurinnsis, Rome, 1956, 151.

18 Holy Week, Interim Text, English Translation, Third Edition, Wellington, 2010, 268.

SEVEN

CONSIDERATIONS

Our liturgical responses during Covid-19's lockdowns have left us with critical theological-liturgical questions concerning the place of the baptised as a constitutive element of the act of worship. It has left us wondering if the Mass isn't primarily a clerical activity, despite what we might say. The following seven considerations attempt to summarise the experience and the questions it raises. Some are presented as statements and others as questions for your reflection.

1: The Need for the Sacred

Today, in the world of Covid-19, we experience the raw need for sacramental life and eucharistic communion and Grace. Covid has brought a layer of grief that, like volcanic ash, settles upon the landscape and changes the chemistry of the soil. Every decision is tinged with grief, from taking a mask to the supermarket to deciding who can attend a family funeral of 50 or 100 guests. Grief upon grief comes with the loss of income, jobs, businesses, physical interaction, personal freedoms, and more. How do we address this when we cannot celebrate and gather sacramentally? The answer is too simple—we can't! And there is the most profound grief of all—we have no access to our sacramental life through the official sacramental mediation, so we must improvise.

The Church lives out of the celebration of the sacraments, and the Eucharist is source and summit, but what becomes of us when sacraments are inaccessible? Is our need for the Mass the same as our need for Eucharist, or are we able to celebrate Mass without actually caring about Eucharist? Can we distinguish between the two to understand our own motivations? The point of the question is: has the need to hear and say Mass overridden the purpose of eucharistic praise and thanksgiving? Is there a moment when one must say that liturgy has a quality that online or virtual mass cannot attain? Is it reasonable to suggest that liturgy can only be enacted, celebrated, participated in when it is physical and in this sense "real" and that virtual and online worship of whatever type is never the liturgy?

This is dangerous ground because I could give the impression that I am doubting the Mass, the sacraments, and the priesthood in whatever form they are performed. I am not, but I am asking: are we using these as performance tools to avoid the suffering that comes with the loss of our mediated sacramental system? I admit it is a fine line distinguishing between the "saying of Mass" and the "celebrating of the Eucharist", but I ask it because I am concerned that where praise becomes functional, it loses its transformational quality. It is true that people devotedly "hear" Mass and priests devotedly "say" Mass, but I think these two forms of "hearing" and "saying" belie a functional approach to worship. Equally, people may "celebrate Eucharist" and priests "preside at Eucharist" without a transformative mentality or awareness. Nevertheless, I think that to "celebrate Eucharist" and "preside at Eucharist" are more likely to be transformative than transactional.

Have the motivations behind our decision to turn to artificial forms of the Mass negatively impacted our understanding of the Eucharist? Is our move to artificial forms an instance of our collective inability to suffer the loss of the sacraments during the lockdown and our refusal to live the experience of loss and suffering? As a result of online worship, have we come to know better the Eucharist's nature, how it functions, what it celebrates, and the context of celebration that makes it meaningful? Similarly, the motivations that led some clergy to commit the liturgical abuses of the drive-through and walk-up communion need to be seen as the reflection of something larger. Is this behaviour indicative of a reversion to pre-conciliar thinking, or is it an uncovering of the still operative theology of priesthood and ministry that has never been reformed following the Council? Have our initiatives in online worship, zoom meetings, and the like been motivated by the need for parishes and clergy to communicate their value and worth, not just celebrate the Paschal Mystery?

The religious and faith motivations we express in liturgy, sacraments, and ecclesial life are the tips of a deeper reality. While we fight over these expressions, they are not our key motivations. To discern our motivations, we need to look at our deeper religious needs, fears, and consolation, which are complex and often conflicted. For example, healthy piety, spirituality, personal need and psychology, faith, and closer union with God conflict with eschatological fear, group and personal psychosis, infantilised belief, popular religious purity, and co-dependency. At the heart of every individual's search for God is their struggle to articulate their image or understanding of God and how salvation or redemption works for them. The power of the God-salvation image is seen in the refusal to be vaccinated and the demands for communion on the tongue and from the chalice. It is in the demand for women deacons and priests and the international trafficking of priests and seminarians. It is in popular religiosity that thinks another rosary will get a resident's visa. It is in the desire to create a sustainable priestless church and more. The God-salvation image is not a "pure" form of reality, though many think it is. It is a personal experience mediated through the expressions of liturgy, sacraments, and ecclesiology that belong to the individual and do not necessarily reflect the theology of the Church.

The need for the Mass has seen us neglect or not nurture other forms of prayer like the Lectio Divina and liturgies of scripture. Did we not take these forms online because we know their natural habitat is the small group or the private room, or did we not use them because they are less than the Mass? Are they less valuable forms of pray because they are not looped into the God-salvation feeling we get from the Mass?

2: The Consumption of Worship

The denial of deprivation and the demand for Mass fuelled our consumerist approach to religion to the point that we turned the Eucharist into a product rather than address the critical theological question of deprivation. We justified our consumerist liturgical approach along the lines "if we can do it, we will!". Our need to be seen to contribute as a faith community was a strong motivation for virtual masses and pastoral outreach. Doing nothing was not an option. We wanted to communicate and connect with our parishioner base the same way businesses wished to communicate with their customers. Perhaps being caught in a consumer-shopkeeper relationship is the hallmark of modern parish life?

However, seeing the Mass as a product for consumption lies beneath many justifications of liturgical abuses such as the walk-up communions, drive-in reconciliations, and drive-up communions. The productive element of the Mass is an expression of the presumptive theology of the Mass: first, as a function of the Church; second, as a function of the priesthood; and third, as a personal devotional practice of clerics. The productive mentality also underscores the Decree issued by the Vatican during the lockdown.

The virtual experience of Mass was all that some needed and created, giving the virtual church a new platform and a new sense of evangelization. Digital platforms have become the new tool for evangelisation without a reliable theology of technology. These new platforms created international communities of parishioners and a new sense of connection to the world church.

In some places, virtual prayer groups flourished, but not to the same extent as the virtual Mass. These prayer groups relied on an already existing network. They relied primarily on the scriptures, personal sharing, and shared prayer. They "democratized" worship further because they were led by lay presiders using official and non-official texts. But one cannot forget the joke that tells the more profound truth: "Darling, where's the remote? I need to fast-forward the Mass!" "Hey, can you freeze-frame Father? I need a coffee!" Jokes reflect a more profound truth and the actual state of our worship. Mass-surfing, "presiding" alone and communion separated from Mass all beg the question: why did we do this?

What drove our consumption? Why did we go to the online church bakery to watch the baker baking bread we could never eat? Why was "window-shopping" the Mass seen as an authentic form of prayer? Is our response, in wealthy countries, linked to presumptions of power, production, consumption and greed? Is this why we could treat our most sacred act as a commodity?

3: Community and Communication

I think we are a more vital local church now and have a better sense of community after the experience of Covid than before. How do I judge this? By the participation levels and the willingness of people to engage and support each other. In August 2021, we re-established the Parish Telephone Tree in our second major lockdown. We introduced "Prayer and Coffee" each Wednesday at 4 pm, which drew 40–60 participants each time for a brief prayer time and conversation.

In most parishes, the works of the parish rely on the participation of a consistent, small group of very active people. Covid has forced us—and many parishes—to reach out to the edges of the parish and communicate in various ways. Staying in touch is critical! It appears that the inability to celebrate the Eucharist together during lockdown has both disrupted our gathering and made it more meaningful. For a time, we were all non-practising Catholics, in that we were all freed of the requirement to attend Sunday Mass and unable to attend Mass and receive the sacraments. The implications of this are only beginning to emerge.

The lockdown experience was different for each person. Technologically, it brought to light the difference between older and younger Catholics and how they use the internet and online formats. Still, surprisingly it revealed that positive and negative attitudes towards online worship are not generationally linked. One cannot conclude that older parishioners are less able to access online communities than younger parishioners or are less inclined to form online communities. Generally, older parishioners join the online events and prayer times. They seem to value this more than younger parishioners.

Domestic prayer has sustained many families during the lockdown, and parents took on the role of the presider, with their children as integral participants. Many people prayed on their own or with neighbours—literally—over the fence. Forgetting these experiences could widen the division between the church's "official" prayer and "home prayer". Integrating the domestic church's experience into Sunday liturgy will probably mean a reconsideration of the form of the Liturgy of the Word. Many parishioners found resources for nourishing their faith that they continue to use, and there is greater freedom from the obligation to attend Mass that was not previously obvious.

The Covid response in places like New Zealand has clearly shown that religious life is not a highly valued element of our social and political life. The priest's life has been tested through the experience of being a non-essential worker and a non-front-line worker in countries like Aotearoa New Zealand. The experience of clergy celebrating the Eucharist without the presence of the community cannot be overlooked because it is integral to any consideration of the nature of the Eucharist and priesthood. However, we must not forget that the clergy have suffered the impact of liturgical and social lockdown. As men and believers, pastors, and clerics, they have responded to a profound experience of constraint. For many, this led them online, in a genuine attempt to maintain contact with parishioners and keep the Church's face present in the life of believers and the world.

4: A Transactional Mindset

The impact of transactional thinking on liturgical practice is evident in the way we have gone about liturgy up to lockdown and why our lockdown solutions were essentially transactional. The transactional mindset is present in the "return to business-as-usual" approach as we emerge from lockdown. The transactional mindset presumes that salvation is impossible without the established habitual parish life and worship patterns. Based on this, it presumes that emerging from lockdown is just another transactional task. It assumes there is no post-traumatic impact, even when it is evident that set, habitual patterns of Catholicism are breaking down.

The transactional mindset is characterised by the "I want what I want" attitude. It is also popularist, and when what is demanded is not given, it is seen as a denial of individual rights. This attitude is evident when individuals demand tongue communion and cannot accept the rationale for refusing during a pandemic. It is seen in the decisions of priests who have celebrated multiple Sunday masses during restrictions thinking that the availability of the Mass is more than its quality. The transactional mindset is evident in parishioners whose approach to Mass is to "dine and dash". They resent the use of music and singing as an imposition. In these instances, the transaction is more important than the meaning of the liturgy itself. Transaction masquerades as an attitude of reverence when it is a sign of protest.

The notion of the transaction is part of the history of Catholicism and the Mass. The mass offering and the sale of indulgences attest to this. While this general form of transaction plays a role, the more critical aspect is how prayer is used, liturgically, as a means of transacting Grace, redemption, or reconciliation with God. It is not uncommon to see Catholics using prayer and sacraments like reconciliation as bargaining chips; "if you give me this God, I will give you that."

Praying *in order to* get something in return illustrates the notion of transactional worship and belief. It is an ancient human practice to use worship to appease divinity and get something out of God. Where religious and liturgical participation is built on the notion of God as the giver or the denier of things one needs, prayer becomes the means to the end. For example, praying two rosaries more a day or attending an additional weekday Mass in order to pass an exam or get a visa shows that the exam and the visa are desired objects. In this instance, God and liturgy are just the means to that end. While God is undoubtedly prayed to, the object of desire is the positive exam result or the work visa, not the glorification of God *per se.* It is not that prayer or good works are wrong, but how they are used. The problem here is the transactional mindset and its ultimate disappointment.

Transactional prayer forms are observable in all forms of cultural Catholicism. In popular piety and religiosity, forms of superstition are highly manipulative. For example, individuals are told to pray using an incantational form of words and wear particular pieces of sacred clothing, so God will give them what they ask for. Superstitious thinking takes the form of words and the clothing beyond the ceremonial or pious, where the clothing and the words become instrumental to the ability of the divinity to act. At this point, one is dealing with magic. When God does not "play ball" in this magic interchange, either God is too busy, did not hear correctly or has another plan in mind. Thus, we create a scenario where the prayer is not wasted but not prayed at the right time. In a more sinister world, the failure of God to act is based on the weakness of the magic or on God's desire that the petitioner needs to suffer more.

Transactional forms of prayer develop their own vocabulary, and it becomes central to the ritual practices. Common words often need to be replaced by "sacred" words because the ordinary is not good enough, so sacred words are invented or taken over from common usage. They are given a sanctified form and are defended as holy words that have—quasi in themselves—a transcendent quality. Such words become part of the sacred vocabulary and code words for particular ecclesial groups. Thus, a previously intelligible word is rendered unintelligible to ensure that the sacral language keeps its meaning and security.

Transactional religion takes elements like language and ethnicity from their original context and uses them in the religious world, where they function in the *cultus* of worship. As the cultural elements go through the process of becoming religious-cultic forms, they are invested with religious meaning such as who is God, how does God operate, what is salvation, and how is it achieved or lost? These religious-cultic forms are then ritualised through vesture, language, song, music, posture, and gesture and become ritual forms. The ritualised forms are then used to transact powerful social understandings of gender, age, sexuality, race, and language. Religious-social constructs justify social inclusion or exclusion. In sacral cultures—those that presume a deity or deities—religious and social cultures legitimise each other through religious and political practices and institutions. They become so interrelated that they are synonymous, creating a "default" religious-political world one submits, subscribes to, or resists.

5: Active and Conscious Presence

Active participation is the Pauline liturgy's simple and powerful organisational idea that frames the Church at worship. Active participation in worship is an internal and external experience. For example, in the Mass, an individual's inner participation in the Eucharist is expressed outwardly in their physical presence, hearing the Word of God, praying, singing, and receiving communion. Active participation is *Sacrosanctum Concilium*'s central organisational principle for Catholic liturgy. It is the principle that must be applied to the act of worship because it articulates the interrelationships of space, place, movement, ritual, presence, assembly, and ministers. With its subsidiary principle Noble Simplicity, active participation moderates liturgical arts, architecture, vesture, music, posture, and gesture.

Active participation is the foundation of the presence of the People of God in the liturgy. Active participation frames the liturgical act as a mediated liturgical act in which both the laity and clergy are equal participants. Thus, in the broadest possible meaning, active participation allows us to speak of the con-celebration of the sacraments by all the assembly. It enables us to talk of the presider—in a qualified sense—as a participant in liturgy, as he too hears the Word, sings, and prays along with everyone else.

The loss of active participation by the laity in worship is not moot. We have seen it happen, and this loss brings confusion to the post-conciliar liturgical rites. It forces us to ask why bishops and priests actively facilitated this loss and why the laity joined in. I believe there are two reasons for this. First, an erroneous misreading of the nature of active participation as a spiritual activity or activism in the liturgy (a job for everyone), and second, the influence of the thinking of the pre-conciliar rites where the laity was not essential to Mass. These two reasons, present throughout the liturgical lockdown, have contributed to what I would describe as participatory confusion. But they were present in liturgical practices before 2020.

The less than adequate understanding of authentic liturgical participation has given us the visuals of priests performing all lay ministries, even where lay members are present. The erroneous reading of active participation and its pre-conciliar thinking has produced the virtual Mass, drive-through confessions and walk-up holy communion. Ironically it is also at play where the priests and online viewers have shared the Words of Institution or when the priest has telephonically "consecrated" bread and wine.

The crisis of physical liturgical presence is a crisis of active, liturgical participation. The questions raised are critical for the post-conciliar Pauline Liturgy (1970) because it presumes conscious, active participation by all the faithful in the liturgical act. It is the bedrock of the theology of the church that is articulated in the liturgy. The reversion to pre-conciliar thinking and actions has revealed the depth of the crisis of post-conciliar liturgical practice.

6: Communion Ecclesiology

Vatican II's understanding of the mission and nature of the church is reflected in its communion ecclesiology. In key conciliar documents, the theological meaning and purpose of the People of God are expressed as an ecclesiology of believers, not as a cleric hierarchy. The fourth chapter of *Lumen Gentium* is an excellent example.

The Council's ecclesiology, articulated in *Sacrosanctum Concilium*, is: 'for the liturgy, through which "the work of our redemption takes place, especially in the divine sacrifice of the Eucharist", enables the faithful to make this relationship present in their lives'.[1] This affirms the relationship between worship, church, and belief, making possible the theology of the four liturgical presences of Christ in the liturgy.[2]

Liturgy is the Church's public act 'performed by the mystical body of Jesus Christ, that is, by the Head and his members' to which all the baptised belong. The Dogmatic Constitution on the Church (11) takes this up where it states that sacraments give structure to the sacred and express it in an organic priestly communion. The liturgy's place in the Church's life is affirmed in holy scripture and the earliest writings of the ancient church. Based on this witness, the Church teaches that the liturgy is 'an exercise of the priestly office of Jesus Christ'. Liturgy is where 'the sanctification of women and men' is expressed in symbols.

Sacrosanctum Concilium 10 reminds us that to 'praise to God in the midst of his church, to take part in the sacrifice and to eat the Lord's supper' is the summit of the Church's activity. At the same time, number 12 reminds us it is not the only liturgical activity of the Church. For the Second Vatican Council, the pre-eminent expression of the Church at worship is in the full, conscious, and active participation of all God's people. This forms the basis of the relationship between prayer and belief (the lex orandi and the lex credendi).

We are at a turning point—the liturgical axial age—because we no longer fully understand the relationship between public prayer, belief, *kerygma*, and *communio* in the practice of liturgy. The breakdown in our understanding of the relationship between these elements has produced "liturgy" that fails to proclaim the Paschal Mystery. Rather than enabling "the faithful…to express in their lives and manifest to others the mystery of Christ and the real nature of the true Church",[3] we are impeding this. It fails to be leitourgia because it is an inauthentic articulation of the unity of the Eucharist's experiential and ontological elements. Because we could not gather in physical fellowship— and were not prepared to wait—our solution was to separate the ontological and experiential dimensions of the Eucharist from each other through separating them liturgically.

The online community has become more widespread in church circles than before lockdown. It is here to stay in one form or another. Those, like me, who see the online or virtual Mass as the antithesis of Eucharist's most profound meaning and purpose are challenged by those who disagree. Where they see new ways to widen communion and become more relevant and engaged through online masses, I see a reduction in the meaning of the Eucharist and a further commodification of sacramental mediation. I do not see a problem with relevance, engagement, or connection through online prayer forms. Still, I do not think the online Mass or virtual Eucharist is the way to do this.

7: Sacramental Mediation

After a team discussion concerning online masses and a request for online exposition, a co-worker who worships at a local evangelical church said to me, "I honestly don't understand how you Catholics have got from the simplicity of a gathering "doing this in memory of me" to a place of paralysis, where you need to create an online eucharist that no one wants".

The reason for the discussion circled our sacramental system's relationship between sacramental mediation and sacramental reception. Catholic theology has always maintained the sacramental principle that everything can embody and communicate the divine. Our sacramental system is based on the mediation principle that sacraments are corporate and communal and mediated by the ordained minister through the Church. Sacraments are not transactions of Grace in a commercial sense; they are relational expressions in sign and symbol that discloses the divinity. They are acts of the priesthood of Christ through which the Church responds to God in worship.

Sacraments are, immediately, acts of the Church that reveal the nature and mission of the Church [we have also maintained the distinction between ministry and mission]. In the liturgical-sacramental rites, the Church becomes most herself. As mediated signs, sacraments express worship in liturgy. They are our participation in Christ's worship of the Father and signs of unity and Christ's presence. The lasting effect of every sacrament is to be in relationship with the Church.

Sacraments are always mediated to an individual by another member of the Church and rely on the minister's and recipient's intentions because they are not magic. The minister acts in the name of Christ and the Church doing what the Church intends from the sacramental act—the epiphany of God's presence. Because the sacraments are acts of the Church and not individuals' personal acts of devotion or piety, the minister's role is essential as the presider of the community's/Church's sacraments. These are given to a recipient from and within the Church.

But neither is the recipient a passive participant. A fruitful reception—rather than a valid one—relies on the recipient's disposition. Reception of a sacrament draws an individual more fully into the life and mission of the Church, but a sacrament cannot have an ecclesial impact or expression if the recipient does not share the faith of the Church or believe in the reality the sacramental-liturgical rite symbolises. When received as intended, the sacraments impart Grace through the liturgical rites, which open the recipient and the whole community to receive this Grace in a way that makes it come alive and active in worship and works of charity.[4]

But what does all this theology mean if sacramental mediation is itself compromised? What is the point of a mediated sacramental system, with its fabulous theology, if it cannot be accessed in practice? Similarly: what is the point of having a car parked in the garage if the only person who can legally, intentionally and ritually drive it is locked inside the house?

---

1 SC., 2, 117.
2 SC., 7, 120.
3 SC., 2, 117.
4 See, SC., 59.

NO CONCLUSION
YET

It is December 2021 as I write this conclusion. We have celebrated the Christmas Season in our new "traffic light system" for vaccinated congregations and have additional masses for non-vaccinated congregants.

I do not want to draw conclusions because Covid-19 is an ongoing reality. Like others, we have experienced having our churches closed to all people, our sacraments suspended, and funerals of parishioners without clergy. In 2021 we have noticed a considerable drop in our Mass attendance numbers. With restrictions of 100 people per Mass, we are seeing an average mass attendance of 60 people.

Our experience of social and liturgical lockdown has been short compared with others, and some will critique my analysis based on the brevity of the experience; no one is untouched by the experience of Covid-19. In 2020, once we emerged from social lockdown, the "new normal" began to look much like the "old normal", though with subtle differences. In 2021 the return was different. The "new normal" differed because parishioners were more reluctant to return to Sunday Mass and parish functions than in 2020. This might be accounted for in part by the nature of the Delta variant. The fall-off in numbers in 2021 was across the age range, and the most noticeable absence was children and young families. In 2021 we saw a greater take-up of home worship and greater self-reliance on personal worship forms. There are three words that I would offer to summarise what I have experienced and what I have seen in others; tedium, grief, and hope.

Tedium is the tiredness that inhabits every day and every decision. We are living in the tedium of a car journey that won't end where everyone, not just the children, is asking, "are we there yet?"

Living in the banality of sameness, in a routine of masks and indecision, is tedious. There is a wearisomeness in the lives of many. I can see it on their faces; it falls like a pall over events that would otherwise be joyous. There's a tiredness to deciding, again and again, not to do something, not to go somewhere, not to visit someone, not to come to church. The tedium of figuring out again and again what still makes sense seeps into bones and spirit.

Grief, like volcanic ash, has layered itself over our living. No decision is without it. The grief of doubt: will it happen? The grief of peace: will we lose it? The grief of loss: will we get back what is gone? The grief of death: shall we bury or cremate? The grief of freedom: what can we be sure of? Each decision and ordinary daily tasks are layered with grief. The tedium of grief consumes energy. It leaves individuals, organizations and businesses open one day and closed the next. Grief goes deep into the psyche and manifests itself in violence, avoidance, and withdrawal. Grief sets up opposing points of view that demand attention and defies reconciliation.

We have experienced the most significant reformation of Catholic liturgy through liturgical lockdown since Vatican II, and I have only sketched some implications of the sustaining technologies we have applied to it. Covid has exposed the more profound, unresolved challenges of liturgy and church we have been avoiding for decades. Of course, reformation is a loaded word, yet that is what we have experienced. In a matter of weeks, the pandemic did something no pope, bishop, priest, or despot could do: it shut down churches across the globe and made people reach for other forms of worship and community.

Covid is the crisis that brings everything to the point of unstoppable change. The pandemic experience is a reforming experience that reconfigures our presumptions of contemporary life. For example, international travel has been the hallmark of freedom for many people. I remember when those living behind the Iron Curtain were not permitted to travel, and we on the "free side" saw this as a limitation on their freedom. Now we cannot travel freely or safely, and our worldview has been reformed.

For the Church, too, the constraints imposed through social lockdown have reformed the way we view ourselves, and this will contribute to ongoing ecclesial changes in ways we can only guess at now. In this experience, which is both social and liturgical, we have lost our access to the sacred physical space, whether that space is a park, a church, a home visit or a café. And, in the liturgy, we have lost the presence of the laity in the sacred liturgical space.

In the face of crisis, priests and people turned to online media to maintain our sacramental and pastoral world. Moving the Mass online into the virtual environment was a work-around, as were drive-through communion stalls and telephone reconciliations. Equally, online prayer times, downloadable and take-home liturgies were workarounds. These forms "kept the shop open and the lights on", which is not bad. These sustaining technologies kept the mainstream parishioners happy, but they were not satisfying.

Virtual masses, telephone reconciliation, and zoom anointings are not the answer, but they will remain and be used as sustaining technologies while the truly disruptive percolates underneath. The days of exclusive sacramental mediation by those in Holy Orders may be more limited than we think.

Although the need for community and the desire to gather for prayer have driven these initiatives, the responses reveal both the limitations of a mediated sacramental system and the opportunities for a shared, inclusive understanding of worship. Key questions arise from this experience concerning the meaning of the word liturgy. Is liturgy only connected to the celebration of the sacraments, or can it also describe non-sacrament prayer times? The use of home-Eucharists and the greater reliance on "mum and dad presiders" has asked how we operate a mediated sacramental system when the mediators are locked in their houses. More critically: who can be a priest?

Globally, Covid has brought our sacramental system to a grinding halt. All our initiatives begin from this reality because our experience of Covid was one of sacramental and pastoral deprivation.

The value of a mediated sacramental system is its communal experience of prayer. The limitation of this system is seen where only a specific group of people can minister those sacraments to others, in our case, celibate, unmarried men. The experience of being Catholic was changed for many, and we all became—as one colleague commented—non-practising Catholics. The experience of sacramental deprivation throughout Covid was acute for most Catholics but not a new reality for millions. Before Covid, many churches lacked sufficient priests to maintain effective pastoral ministry. This is likely to continue because many churches, like ours, will no longer import priests or seminarians.

Just as Covid has impacted the sacrament of the Eucharist and the celebration of the Mass, it will change the way we celebrate the other sacraments and the priesthood. Without wanting to conflate the "ordinary" situation of priest-shortage before Covid with the "extraordinary" situation during Covid, I think the experience of Covid has the potential to help us resolve the "ordinary" crisis of the shortage of priests. What follows Covid is not yet clear, but we need to consider the limitations of sacramental mediation exclusively through the ordained. There are risks associated with this line of thought. However, the restrictions on the availability of international priests as a result of Covid will contribute to further clergy shortages and debates regarding the future functioning of the parish system. Covid did not create the problem of clergy shortages. Instead, it has captured in a snapshot a decades-long problem.

The classification of church services as public health and safety risks and the classification of the clergy as "non-essential" workers give an insight into the New Zealand political view of religion. The use of civic and legal prohibitions against church gatherings have compromised ordinary pastoral and sacramental life. We need to consider, intelligently, the actual political and social standing of Christianity in general and Catholicism in particular in New Zealand society. The impact of liturgical lockdown demands we consider seriously the limitations of a sacramental system that is—rightly—linked to ordained ministry but which is also compromised through it.

Although online worship assuages our social need for familiar rituals, the loss of liturgical, physical community will be the longest-lasting issue. Once social, physical gatherings became problematic and even dangerous to public health, and social well-being and vaccinations and public access became an issue, it is foolish to think that religious congregations are immune; we are not.

In 2020 when social groups, schools, bars, restaurants, and clubs opened with limited numbers, churches in New Zealand were not allowed to gather because church gatherings were considered a social-health risk. This decision has driven the liturgical reform during Covid because it has marginalised the physical gathering as an unsafe event. As a result, we have reformed the way we celebrate Mass. Now we wear masks, wave at the Sign of Peace, have communion again only under one species, and are physically distanced, or watch it online or don't come at all. All this is already having an undeniable impact on Church ministry and will do so further into the future. Because the liturgical reform through Covid is not finished, there is no conclusion.

Covid has unmasked our operative liturgical theology and practice as transactional. Our transactional understanding of liturgy and priesthood enabled us to turn the Mass into an online product. Before Covid, I heard people talk about "doing liturgy" in the sense of putting "it" together and "going to Church" as a task or chore. Liturgy put together a list of component activities— songs, readings, prayers, notices—and people assigned to "do" them.

Before, Covid liturgy was more of a transaction between the actions that needed to be done and people who had to do them. I sense, now, we are moving away from this transactional approach to worship and pastoral life towards something more transformative. Worship is less judged successful by ritual tasks—songs, actions, gestures, vesture, decoration—and more by the sense of inclusion and participation.

Though, this experience is not true for all. We are still pilgrims finding our way to the Kingdom—sometimes together and sometimes as separate tribes. This has been further complicated by the vaccination issue and the Government's mandate.

Since December 3, 2021, the vaccination mandate has laid another burden on church communities. The Traffic Light System—as it is known—has significant implications for how we gather for Sunday Mass, sacraments and funerals.

The vaccination status of an individual determines if they can attend a public gathering. The number of non-vaccinated attendees reduces to 25 in Red, 50 in Orange, and 100 in Green. Vaccinated attendees are significantly higher (Red 100, Orange and Green unlimited).

This system and the mandating and anger around vaccination have impacted parishes and how they provide for their members, especially on Sundays. It has clarified the social contract at the heart of the liturgical gathering.

We need to use our language around the Mass and the sacraments carefully. It is wrong to describe the Sunday Eucharist as a vaccinated or unvaccinated Mass because it is not a medical or political event. It is also wrong to describe Mass without a vaccine passport as "open", implying that a Mass using a vaccination pass is closed when this is not the case. The distinction between vaccinated and unvaccinated is not theological, so we must avoid using it this way. It has forced us to be careful with our language and not conflate liturgical words with medical and political decisions.

Indeed, congregations already distinguish themselves based on musical and liturgical styles, Sunday Mass times and other preferences. Nevertheless, we must respect the dignity of each person: each person is created in the image of God. From this, an individual's rights and responsibilities flow.

Therefore, it is better to speak of a vaccinated or unvaccinated congregation because this places the onus on each individual attending Mass or a sacramental rite. Individual congregants have the ethical responsibility to attend according to the legal mandate, and they all—including priests— have the obligation not to bring harm or scandal to the liturgical.

As the saying goes, "never let a good crisis pass you by" without taking the opportunity to change, learn and evolve. In the wake of Covid, we need a more robust theology of the liturgical assembly and a theological understanding of the difference between technology in worship and technology for worship. Sadly, we separated the experiential and ontological dimensions of sacraments and liturgy in the virtual masses, like a baker separates the yolk from the albumen. Church leadership is now challenged to consider and contemplate the shape and needs of a post-Covid communal Church.

The liturgical lockdown has given us time to think about the nature of liturgy and its relation to future parish life. There are five mistakes we can make coming back from lockdown if we: (1) ignore the experience of disruption to the domestic church; (2) overlook the clerical response's use of sustaining technologies; (3) do not fully see to understand the new experience of the digital church; and (4) continue seeking a transactional form of worship and ministry. The Chinese proverb, "a person cannot step into the same river twice," tells us that life keeps flowing on, and we will not step back into the church before Covid— those days are gone! We need a new paradigm that Pope Francis's call for a synodal church may supply; the time is ripe for change, but it will be challenging to achieve it without further pruning.

Pope Francis' call for a synodal church marked by co-responsibility, collaboration, and genuine consultation is needed. Still, it is not assured because the success or failure of the synodal approach sits with the bishops and the type of church they want in their dioceses. The synodal process requires that we become a listening church and include all the baptised in the discernment and mission of the Church through participation in Church governance, ministry, and leadership. I do not see this as possible if the laity is not as accepted as a constitutive partner in the liturgical acts of the Church.

Working from the presumption that liturgy is the foundational consideration in all things Catholic, Christian, and theological, I cannot see an ecclesial change of any value or lasting impact that does not first embed in praxis the constitutive liturgical place of the laity in the act of the Church's leitourgia. Only this will ensure the ecclesial culture of subsidiarity, stewardship, and dialogue, enshrined in the Second Vatican II's communion-ecclesiology and missiological, will be operative in the Church.

Change is challenging in every circumstance and for all organisations. Institutions like the Catholic Church do not always deal well with change unless it is in their favour. When it is, they extend their existing structures to transact business-as-usual. When change is against them, institutions resist it because it threatens their power base and market opportunity. How the Church moves forward will be fascinating to watch. But we need to be realistic; most people do not want a renewed Church. They want a church that makes them comfortable and safe—they want actions and technologies that sustain them and do not challenge them to change.

Some will be disappointed that I have not reached a conclusion and not presented a road map for the future. I don't think either is possible because the impact of Covid is only just beginning to show itself. I am sure that online masses will continue as transactional events between clergy and laity in many places. Sadly, their continued use will not further the place and meaning of the laity in the liturgy and in the life of the Church. I think we will continue to see the laity struggle to gain their theological place—as a constitutive element—in the liturgy. And if they cannot find this constitutive place in the liturgy, they will never find it any other part of the Church's life.

In some places, online prayer in the form of a Liturgy of the Word without the eucharistic prayer will evolve and become the norm. In some places, online prayer may be linked with individuals having pre-delivered Holy Communion, like Uber Eats or pizza delivery. It is probable that at-home, online democratised forms of worship that presently exist at the edges of the Church's liturgical life, will, in time, play a disruptive central role to liturgy, priesthood and sacramental mediation. However, I am less sure that the laity will perform at-home eucharist and pray the eucharistic prayer over the bread and wine on their own tables.

So, what is the appropriate response to the liturgical change brought by Covid-19? Will it take us back to the communion theology of the Second Vatican Council and into a Synodal Church, or will it further split the church into digitised and non-digitised rites and traditional and contemporary believers? Will the Covid experience produce a more community-conscious church or a more communication-conscious one? Will the Church's operative theology of liturgy as the preserve of the clergy continue, or will we look for a liturgical praxis that places the laity and the clergy as partners in the act of worship? After Covid, will we better understand the relationship between the sacred physical assembly and its sacred physical space?

In the end, there are more questions than answers. However, I think we will look back at the experience of Covid-19 and see it as an experience of profound social, liturgical and pastoral change. When we reflect on the experience of liturgical lockdown, we will see it as the precursor to change, the initiator of change, and the clarification of change.

Appendix One

Survey One Kotahi Ano

The responses are printed as written

The stress of working online.

Freedom from commitments.
No Mass: priests who put physical health before spiritual health.
Time to share faith with family and be with family.
The feeling of abandonment by men who chose to be shepherds of Christ's flock. A vow is made for better or worse! You cannot just walk away from your responsibilities as a priest. I do not have any trust or respect for this government and feel betrayed by our church leaders. Who is stronger? God or a little germ? Where is your Faith?!
Not being able to get into a church was extremely distressing.
Not being able to attend parish Masses and other activities with other parishioners. It did make me appreciate the 'company' of other parishioners more once we came out of lockdown.
Inability to be with family.
I found it harder to come out of lockdown and re-enter social life than I found lockdown itself.
I am not sure?
Recognition of personal fragility.
Lack of purpose.
Being separated from family.
I disagree with Govt policy and procedure. Around 2% of people who contract COVID die, so 98% of people recover. Those dying are very old or have a co-morbidity. Let's protect the vulnerable and the rest of us carry on living.
Not able to do my own shopping.
Too much produce from my garden to process as I would normally be giving it away!
Time to slow down and evaluate what is important – walks, quiet time, uninterrupted family time.
No impact.
Did not affect me personally.

Inability to receive communion.

Loss of close contact with family and grief at not being able to attend mass and experiencing our Bishops lack of effort to keep churches open. I hear the Muslims did better.

A good time to reflect on one's faith and life in general.

Discovering that the bishops were faithless and failed to follow scripture. I could not find an example of where Jesus shut Himself away from the sick, diseased, or fevered. Not having a Mass and seeing churches closed made me realise how much I believe in the power of the Holy Eucharist and God's Presence in the Church.

Not being able to go to Mass and receive Our Lord or be with Him in the Blessed Sacrament and realising that most (not all) priests and all Bishops valued physical health over spiritual health. Another big impact was to learn that some priests did not understand how important the Sacrifice of the Mass is. Whilst I do not watch tv or YouTube, others reported that some priests sat around their table to offer mass, and others just stopped altogether. This will have serious spiritual repercussions.

Not being able to go to Mass.

No impact on me.

Being unable to work.

I loved being in lockdown and it made me realise that I have had too many commitments that truly aren't all that important. It made me reassess my commitments.

Was the first time I felt safe because an abusive ex-partner couldn't travel into the North Island and unexpectedly turn up. It was a peace I didn't want to end.

Not seeing people face to face.

Nothing.

Quietness and peace.

Didn't have a problem - it needed to be done.

Nothing.

Loss of family contacts.

Loss of daily routine.

No Mass.

Missing Mass at church.

Not able to do own supermarket shopping.

Not being able to attend mass especially Easter celebrations. Inability to visit family.

Stressful.

More appreciative of my religion.

Inconvenience and lost holiday experiences. Some friendships were difficult to sustain and had to go back to the start with building some relationships.

Being unable to attend Eucharist.

It gave me time to stop and assess how hectic my life was and how much time I spend out of the home. It highlighted for me that my school-aged child probably only had a couple of years remaining at home, and that I was missing time with family that I would never get back once all the children had left home. Consequently, I have given up activities that took me out of home the most, and I am glad that I did it. For this, I thank Covid.

Being on my own, lack of physical social contact.

Isolation away from family and friends.

Difficult to get going after lockdown.

Losing loved ones and being able to farewell them properly.

Not being able to receive the Eucharist physically and to be with fellow parishioners.

Working from home. I prefer to work at work and do my personal living at home.

A time for personal reflection.

I have slowed down. More reflective. Unsure if lazy or realistic for my age (75).

Separated from mokopuna.

No major issues as retired and in good health. Instead of visitation of the sick & vulnerable we were still able to support them by phone and address needs.

Disruption to church participation.

Tough during special time of lent.

Uncertainty and reduced confidence in political leadership and authority, unable to trust what we are told in the media. Unable to see a positive outcome. Vaccines give false hope of cure – new diseases always on the horizon.

I was so sad to see people too scared to even look at each other, let alone smile when out at the supermarket or walking. To me people seemed to withdraw into themselves. For me it was the loss of physical time with friends – just even to have a cuppa. It was isolating!!

Had to work from home. Could not go out. Had much more conversation with others by other than face to face. This was positive.

My parents were planning on retiring shortly after the lockdown started. The Covid lockdown effectively brought this forward, and I struggled with them being home so much more.

Lack of mobility. Having to look after grandchildren week about through the lockdown because parents worked in essential services. I was tired by the time they went back to school. I missed my friends but got to appreciate the length my son went too to reassure my sister who lives on her own stresses about things.

Not being with my community.

No great impact.

The companionships of the parishioners. Not being able to receive the Sacraments.

Loss of my income.

Although I never labelled it as such at the time as Samaritan, but rather it's just 'me', 'who I am'. Grocery shopping for those unable to, preparing meals for elderly neighbours, letterbox drop offs of goodies on my walks. I became more aware of community outside family. My religious spiritual needs were not met by online Mass, which I quickly stopped watching or put on long pause, but in part replaced by my daily walks and musings; my new spiritualness. Fasting from the Eucharist was a reality I accepted, but a reality I became annoyed at when I watched the Priests on-line seemingly to think they could Eat and Drink of the Eucharist "on my behalf". I don't think so ! My faith is more than COVID!

Not being able to physically attend Sunday Mass.

Not being able/required to play for Mass, I began to re-evaluate my own input within the worship community. I found that my own relationship with God and particularly our Blessed Mother Mary was strengthened considerably. Being able to participate in Mass online was at first a forced experience. I persevered with it and after some weeks under Level 4 restrictions I found myself more spiritually aware of the mystery in which I was invited by the celebrant to become an online witness/participant. To experience something of what it was like for those first followers of Jesus, locked in the upper room out of fear—I felt that I came to identify with that in a profound new way in Easter of 2020. (Obviously not under Roman tyranny but hemmed in by an unseen threat.) I attended Mass online in Wanganui, Palmerston North, Plimmerton, Australia, and Boston. In the case of the last two I wanted to know how the wider worship community offshore was handling the lockdown in their Sunday worship. I had a front-row seat at every Mass!... so missed nothing. I could increase the volume to hear the priest, or minister clearly. The spiritual communion—instead of physically being present to receive the precious Body and Blood ... yes, that remains very important. I have to say that it remains an unresolved issue of lockdown restrictions for me.

Income was okay, some improved relationships within the household.

I have become a bit of a hermit.

Settling from a reasonably busy life in the community to being more confined. The greatest benefit was a return to closer contact with neighbours as no one went to work and there was time to stop and chat.

Increased paperwork, inefficient work means (so longer hours and reduced productivity) drastic income reduction, other ways more time with family and fantastic to have break in usual routines and wonder at why God chose me to be in NZ and have a relative heaven compared to the rest of the world, i.e., huge gratitude, loved the lovely Autumn weather, reduced cars, more birds, and New Zealanders focus away from consumerism. It was overall a blessed time for us.

Apart from not being able to attend Mass found time to catch up by phone and facetime with family friends and fellow parishioners some of whom I had never met.

The silence was magnificent! Technology kept people close. People looked after each other more.

Not being able to see, socialise and show usual affection with family, parishioners, and friends.

Not having the sacraments, otherwise managed well.

Inability to travel or attend a couple important family occasions. Disappointed for young adult children who had planned to travel internationally.

A deeper sense of humility and trust in the Lord.

The uncertainty of each day– note lockdowns

Survey Two CathNews Survey

The responses are printed as written

More time for prayer and reflection.

Not receiving the Body (and Blood) of our Lord Jesus Christ.

Unable to attend daily Mass.

I felt divorced from my parish. I was really grateful for my prayer group (not parish-based), which continued online. Through work, I received the bishops' communications and access to some great online websites!

The continuing uncertainty.

Not being able to go to church.

More time to myself.

Not being able to attend Mass in my Parish on Sunday.

Nothing really. It was what it was. I just accepted the decisions made to protect the country but felt Church leaders (not only Catholic) did not speak out quickly or forcefully enough to Government to allow Churches to be acknowledged as essential services.

I had to think outside the box and think about others as well. It was a strange but inspiring experience.

Showed the fragility of our life—religiously, socially, fiscally. Showed me that we take so much for granted. What are the important realities in our life?

Opened our minds and hearts to new ways of being church - breaking the clericalism mould.

Disruption. Added an element of fear, uncertainty, and vulnerability to my being.

Shock at gutlessness of hierarchy.

Not being able to receive Holy Communion.

Stress and anxiety.

Realisation that I must be content with what I have.

Miss praying together then mixing together. Both important.

Showed up lazy bishops who closed churches when 100 people were allowed to go.

Not receiving the Eucharist.

I felt and was supported. Just a bit lonely at times, missing the social presence of friends but happy to do my part.

I was left to look after my two pre-schoolers by myself. My husband was an essential worker who worked extremely long hours leaving me to shoulder most of it all alone with no support and abandoned by our priests and bishops who provided no spiritual support during such a tough time. My mental illness that I was successfully managing came up again and I got anxiety. It was a horrid time that I wonder how I ever survived.

Re-asses "what's important".

Missed attending mass with a congregation but was glad we could watch it online at the time.

Not being able to have family support with my young child.

Not being able to spend time with my family.

Anxiety.

Missing face-to-face community involvement. but being able to form small telephone clusters to keep in touch with fellow parishioners.

Not being able to see my family face to face. They all live in the UK. and I was supposed to visit in July 2020. Not knowing when I will see them again in person, especially the older ones is very frightening. I would normally see them every two years.

Nothing much: a great opportunity for some space for reflection with no responsibilities or pressures.

No Holy Communion.

I lost my social network.

Not being able to go to Mass and join in with community.

I was distraught that I could not celebrate Lent, Holy Week and Easter at church – but this motivated me to implement a set of personal devotions to help me enter into these liturgical seasons even without the benefit of regular church attendance. As a result, I have become better informed about my faith, and my spiritual life has flourished - an unexpected but very welcome effect of the lockdown!

The lack of a coordinated, reasonable, logical response by the Diocese was deeply disappointing and my faith suffered a number of setbacks as a result. The lack of technical expertise was also embarrassing.

Intense prayerfulness.

I had more time to increase my spiritual input.

Returning to a half-empty church, familiar faces no longer present, no life in our church. Sometimes wondering why, I even bothered to attend as it was like boring ritual. A growing awareness that going to Mass no longer held the same importance for me. Something has to change as our generation's needs are not being met. (I have been very active in the Church for 50 years.)

Loss of community. Sense of unity, which is the plan of God – Eph. 1: 10.

Working from home.

When we first went into lockdown my 30-something son wouldn't let me do our own grocery shopping as I am just over 70. Having my children tell me what I can and can't do makes me feel old!

I missed parish celebrations of the Eucharist with the parish community.

More time for quiet personal prayer; I got some academic work done which required concentration and time; I enjoyed the lockdowns.

Loss of interaction with parish family and regular Mass; time and leisure for peaceful reflection on life and my responsibilities.

I had a complete change of lifestyle during/after lockdown to take daily time out for walk/run and prayer. To learn to focus on the priorities. To be able to watch Masses (especially Easter Vigil) with Germany online was very moving and special for me and the family as we do not have the change. Also, the parishes made it amazingly enjoyable and sacred (candles, light, darkness – not just switching on a light like here). During Lent I watched daily Mass in the Black Forest, sometimes from the Cathedral or from a small church (where I know the priest from earlier times). Also work-wise (School Pastoral Ministry) the lockdown was a great teaching experience. We switched to a YouTube Chapel over night with daily school prayer, liturgy, google-meet Masses and Liturgies. It made us creative and moving with our students whatever they needed. It lasts until today; we had, for example, black ribbons for Ash Wednesday, as we couldn't do ashes. The whole experience was very empowering and special.

More individual than a sense of community, the Body of Christ.

It especially made me question priesthood/clericalism – why is it exclusively male, celibate, lifelong?

Loss of persons contact and Sunday Eucharist together.

I felt well supported here in my Townhouse and felt connected with the Parish through the online Masses. This was new for our Parish. It is great for those unable to get to Mass. e.g., elderly parishioners and those with disability.

Feeling of safety and trust in Jacinda to do the right thing.

The interaction of my church community.

I learnt to work from home, and still deliver pastoral care.

It provoked a re-evaluation of my Catholic identity.

Not being able to participate in the Eucharistic Celebration.

Put on weight but slept more. Enjoyed the peaceful time. Did a couple of online retreats. I am usually a daily Mass goer, so it was a wrench.

A bit of peace and quiet, and a heap more work.

I saved money on petrol. My family were incredibly supportive. My prayer life was improved by some of the you tube offerings around the world.

I became incarcerated in Aotearoa New Zealand – I normally live in Melbourne.

Loved the peace and quiet at home and in the community........plus love shared among those you met.

Non-reception of Eucharist and isolation.

Not being able to visit my close family overseas and in other parts of NZ. Easier to spend time on daily Bible reading, prayer and contemplation but missed Christian Life Community meetings and Services of the Word with Holy Communion.

Not being able to have a funeral for my father. Being isolated from family who live overseas.

I enjoyed to time to rest and reflect. I missed seeing the other parishioners and our happy parish priest.

Become more tolerant.

I missed being able to go to Holy Communion. I missed joining with my sisters and brothers at Mass. I missed the hugs.

Unable to celebrate Easter.

Minimal impact. Greater awareness of person and public health precautions.

It did not change me at all. I still love my God and always will. NOTHING will ever change that! Not even all the changes that are now taking place in my home parish of which I do NOT like! I am NOT pre-Vatican! and cannot adhere to Pre-Vatican!

Loneliness and anxiety with a very busy medical husband, four young kids and none of the external support I usually have. Sense over overwhelmed. Missing loved ones who live in a different island and not seeing them for months.

It was the first time in my life that daily Communion was not available to me if I wanted it. (For six weeks.). It greatly increased my desire to return to daily Communion, which is still not available.

It was hard living alone getting groceries when my workplace insisted that we didn't go to the supermarket. I also find it hard not going to Mass regularly even now as the lockdown levels are usually 1 level higher than everyone else for aged care facilities, so currently level 3 restrictions for my workplace in Christchurch.

I'm retired, so it wasn't a big impact. Spent more time in the garden.

Stopped attending church & had absolutely no personal from the parish at all. Hurtful after 30 years of involvement in the parish. Ex PC chair, been on many committees, led groups, so been very involved.

Concern for family.

It gave me a time of rest and consolidation of my relationship with family.

A feeling of emptiness.

Not much, I am a scholar by preference and with regard to the Liturgy spent many years trying to implement the reforms of Vat 11 until Pope Benedict and his associates reversed the reforms.

Loneliness, separation of family and personal relationships.

Isolation. I was frantically busy but debriefing and relaxing hard on own.

I found I could find God in a more meaningful way at home with my secular family. I felt alone spiritually though and looked forward to frequent txt messages from a priest friend

Appendix Two

Clergy and Liturgical Lockdown

The responses are printed as written

The greatest disruption was the inability to be able to physically visit those who were sick or dying. It was frustrating to not even be able to go to the hospital as Hospital Chaplain and know that our parishioners were dying without the final sacraments and prayers.

No parishioners.

I work with Māori, disruption on lack of personal contact.

The inability to be physically with parishioners.

Meeting people face-to-face and the personal contact of 'normal' (non-virtual) relationships.

Not being able to physically. Inability to gather physically with parishioners and

connect with people.

Isolation from face-to-face contact with my people.

Not being able to visit people.

Low parishioner participation.

No parishioners. A misunderstanding that the priest is a non-essential worker.

Being away from people.

The daily routine of meeting people face-to-face.

Restricted opportunities to visit.

Being unable to physically contact with parishioners, especially

hose who experienced bereavements.

Immediate contact with others.

Not being able to get out to see parishioners and take part in Pastoral outreach in the normal manner.

No social ministry.

Not being out and about and not able to participate as an essential worker.

Not being able to visit and interact with parishioners.

Every activity ceased! e.g., hospital, rest home activity, no funerals. Every Parish activity stopped

Being confined to home.

Inability to move freely.

Lack of good media system, like fibre net, camera, lack of knowledge in movie making or editing, etc.

Being alone.

Very lonely.

Daily life pattern.

There were no disruptions. Rather ministry took different forms.

None.

No disruption.

Zoom meetings.

I live in a rest-home. My opportunities for ministry are very limited.

Only got to see folk in need or special circumstances.

I did not see it as a disruption at all I saw the lockdown during Covid as a fresh challenge for ministry.

No social contact at all.

Visiting the sick was an issue, but later on (Level 3) Rest Homes were obliging for those who were dying. We sent out Parish Newsletters via email, which was well received. There was quite a bit of info that could be communicated. On the whole , I enjoyed 'Lockdown'.

Emphasis on online masses.

Being unable to celebrate Eucharist with the community by far.

Most difficult was not being able to be with people as they were dying and to meet with families when someone died.

Did not celebrate with a dozen or so people in the chapel of the Residential Village.

The inability to gather face to face for Mass and the cancellation of the Easter Triduum.
No mass in the church with parishioners.

Appendix Three

Clergy and Digital Media

The responses are printed as written

Funerals need to be offered to people. Level 4 was sad as funerals were often just burials with no one present. Level 3 had initially 50 people present, then 100. I believe the bishops should have pushed for better recognition of funerals, but, it seemed, that the Prime Minister was not concerned (surely this is to be 'kind'?).

The Church is a very important participant in society and people's spiritual lives need nourishment.

Use of modern technology.

Live with the reality of the present.

The availability of daily Mass in very important for some Catholics.

We can continue to minister to people 'remotely', but with regards to the Mass this may require other who are better with technology to support us.

The Sunday Eucharist is central to parish community life and therefore must be an uplifting worshipping experience for all participating.

It (pandemic) could become the new normal.

We need to be more determined to provide hospital and aged care facility ministry. We failed to make sure that priestly ministry was a "necessary function".

Consider the ways (existing and new) in which parishes can facilitate opportunities for prayer, fellowship, etc.

is it necessary to be together? are we willing to pay the price for it? we need to get our act together.

There are more aspects to this issue than liturgical. These can be brought together and featured through the presentation of the liturgy.

always explain why we do what we do.

Much better preaching and catechesis: why do we do what we do? And why does this really matter?

The experience highlights the importance of the parish keeping contact with parishioners by whatever medium possible, e.g., sending by post or email simple prayer material, sending instructions for the less tech. savvy about viewing Mass online, sending online bulletins, sharing prayer requests.

With our online masses during level 4 we used Zoom Webinar which allowed all sorts of people to participate. In some ways it felt like there was more participation than on a normal Sunday. There was the opportunity to be a bit creative and to enable lay women and men to offer homilies/reflections. I think we need to rethink participation in Sunday Mass and how to engage with people more.

To learn to be at home with technology and the possibilities it offers for ministry and communicating with parishioners and wider audiences such as those in lockdown in other countries.

Use of social media.

Always have the appropriate technology to facilitate communication.

The faithful pray and offer service in all circumstances – even in unexpected and difficult times.

We need to plot our own course not what the Government orders.

Mass is the heart of my faith journey.

The grace of people to pray themselves as family as household or online communications.

Lighten up with regard to mortal sin. Speak as a united Conference for NZ. Sure, the virus was a developing thing, but COMMON sense should have dominated any press release.

Greater use of technology in national and local communication should be developed. Perhaps another dicastery for the NZ Conference could be devised to assist in future Covid like outbreaks?

Help/ teach parishioners how to be patience and love others.

Church structures have to change; parishes are obsolete now.

The learning that took place regarding online 'liturgies' and 'communication' will stand us in good stead.

The most significant enquiry when the restricts were being lifted was when would full Sunday masses be returning and to a lesser degree weekday celebration?

The need for unity among bishops and prompt responses to pastoral need based on sound principles of liturgy and doctrine.

Appendix Four

Priests' view of liturgical disruption

The responses are printed as written

More people are more conscious of being sick and staying at home.

Some people got out of the habit of attending mass. Parish Finances dropped for a period. Parishioners wanting Mass on YouTube, etc.

Good preparation for future serious possible disruptions.

Parishioners not returning.

Loss of parishioners.

Some people stopped coming to Mass during lockdown and have not resumed.

Some people not returning to Mass and people being unsure about receiving Communion under both kinds.

Confusion! The State enunciated the rules with some Catholic cults taking issue. Fancy the NZCBC having to tell everyone that the obligation to miss Mass was lifted! The ongoing chatter which the UK and Irish churches espoused that religion, and the Eucharist was more important that one's health just goes to show how little we have been formed in using our own conscience!

Perhaps a slowdown in Mass attendance?

Some have chosen to continue with on-line Masses, thus not understanding the need for personal presence at Mass. Others have found they have no need to be at Mass.

Many parishioners feel that online Masses are an acceptable substitute for gathering as a community or prefer online masses because of factors such as personal convenience.

Perhaps congregations will be smaller. But perhaps folk will have had to think more deeply as to why they practice, and/or will continue to do so.

A sense of the need to gather in person as being intrinsic to the being Church.

Hard to say. I think it might accelerate the decline in Mass attendance, especially among Europeans.

Parishioners found for themselves resources for nourishing their faith, that they continue to use. This could have resulted in some parishioners who are yet to return to Community celebrations of Eucharist. People still find prayerful support in Masses offered online, from various parts of NZ and the wider world.

Many people stopped coming to Sunday Mass although some have been re-emerging. For some the break became permanent; they probably realised they didn't need it as they managed well enough without Sunday Mass.

I think many people discovered that an online Mass was actually something they felt engaged with. It wasn't just like watching Mass (this surprised me). Many people who couldn't come to Mass prior to lockdown now feel more connected because of the ability to 'participate' in an online Mass.

I think we are stronger as a local church and have a better sense of community and Eucharist and of the need to reach out to those on the edges of the parish through such groups as St. Vincent de Paul, etc.

Not celebrating the eucharist together during that time.

The routine of gathering has been disrupted.

Lots of people have now a freedom about Mass obligation that was not previously amongst regular Mass attenders.

The advent of parishioners viewing Mass online (from anywhere locally or internationally) when they are not able to attend Mass.

Some people have got used to not going to Mass.

Deeper appreciation of life and parish.

A challenge to personal faith.

It brought about (or brought to light?) a bold 'split' between older and younger generations, regarding online events as these categories responded according to their 'default' (online is enough/good substitute; online is not enough).

The longest-lasting impact would have to be communication with parishioners over what is being planned for any further level four liturgical disruption.

A sense of need for hygiene at all times.

Those already on the margins will have lost their already attenuated regular sacramental appreciation and participation.

Is hard to know when we are all back to allow everything be normal.

Loss of confidence in public gatherings and knowing that the state is an excellent deliverer of social care.

Loss of the 'habit' of going to Mass.

Index

Select Bibliography

Church Documents

General Instruction of the Roman Missal in The Roman Missal, English Translation, Third Typical Edition, Wellington (2010).

Code of Canon Law, *Latin – English Edition, New English Translation*, Canon Law Society of America (1999).

Flannery, A., (ed.), *The Basic Sixteen Documents, Vatican II, Constitutions, Decrees, Declarations* (1996).

Books

Beauduin, L., *La Piété de l'Eglise* (1914).

Casel, O., *Das christliche Kultmysterium* (1969).

Christensen, C.M., "The Innovator's Dilemma: When New Technologies Cause Great Firms to Fail" (1997).

Empereur, J., "Models of a Liturgical Theology" in *The Sacraments: Readings in Contemporary Sacramental Theology*, (1981).

Fagerberg, D., *Theologica Prima. What Is Liturgical Theology?* (2004).

Fink, P., 'Sacramental Theology after Vatican II', in P. Fink (ed.): *The New Dictionary of Sacramental Worship* (1990).

Grayland, J.P., *Catholics, Prayer, Belief and Diversity in a Secular Context. A New Zealand Perspective* (2021).

Guardini, R., *Von heiligen Zeichen* (2004).

Guardini, R., *Vom Geist der Liturgie* (1997).

Häußling, A. & Kleinheyer, B. (eds.): *Gottesdienst der Kirche. Handbuch der Liturgiewissenschaft. Gestalt des Gottesdienstes. Sprachliche und nichtsprachliche Ausdrucksform* 3 (1989).

Irwin, K., *Context and Text: Method in Liturgical Theology* (1994).

Kavanagh, A., *On Liturgical Theology: The Hale Memorial Lectures of Seabury-Western Theological Seminary* (1984).

Kasper, W., 'Die Kirche als Sakrament des Geistes', in W. Kasper and G. Sauter (eds.): *Kirche - Ort des Geistes*, (1976).

Lengeling, J. E. in K. Richter (ed.), *Liturgie - Dialog zwischen Gott und Mensch* (1981).

Power, D. N., *Unsearchable Riches: The Symbolic Nature of Liturgy* (1984).

Richter, K., *Gemeinde im Herrenmahl. Zur Praxis der Meßfeier*, (1976).

Richter, K. & Schilson A., *Den Glauben Feiern. Wegeliturgischer Erneuerung* (1989).

Ricoeur, P., *Interpretation Theory: Discourse and the Surplus of Meaning* (1976).

Saliers, D., *The Soul in Paraphrase: Prayer, and the Religious Affections* (1980).

Schmemann, A., 'Liturgical Theology: Remarks on Method', in T. Fisch (ed.): *Liturgy and Tradition. Theological Reflections of Alexander Schmemann*, (1990).

Vorgrimler, H. *Sakramententheologie* (1987).

Articles

Alison, J., "Praying Eucharistically" (2020).

Fransen, P., "Sacraments as Celebrations" *Irish Theological Quarterly* 43 (1976).

Grayland, J. P., "Liturgy is an act of the People of God, and they must be really present. A response to Michael Kelly SJ", La Croix International (2020).

Just, F., "Real Presence and Virtual Liturgies (Part I) A Response to Robert Mickens and J.P. Grayland", La Croix International (2020).

Kelly, M., "Digital Catholicism. The Church needs to reflect deeply on 'virtual' ways to celebrate the faith", *La Croix International* (2020).

Manalo, R., "At the Digital Banquet of the Lord: Part One: A Primer on Livestreamed Mass," *Pastoral Music* (2020).

Rahner, K., "Das neue Bild der Kirche", *Schriften zur Theologie 8* (1968).

Neunheuser, B., "Odo Casel in Retrospect and Prospect", *Worship* 50 (1976).

About the Author

Joseph P. Grayland is a Catholic priest in New Zealand. He has undergraduate degrees in Education and Theology and graduate degrees in History and Theology. He has a Doctorate in Theology from the University of Muenster, Germany and has taught and lectured internationally.

His other books include *It Changed Overnight. Celebrating New Zealand's Liturgical Renewal*, and *Catholics. Prayer, Belief and Diversity in a Secular Context. A New Zealand Perspective*. He has authored numerous articles.

Please check out his Facebook page:
https://www.facebook.com/J-P-Grayland-104789544426434